THE COMPLETE MEXICAN COOKBOOK

1000 Days Of Simple And Drooling Traditional And Modern Recipes For Mexican Cuisine Lovers Full-Color Picture Premium Edition.

ROSEMARIE PIZARRO

EDITOR: LYN   INTERIOR DESIGN: FAIZAN

COVER ART: ABR   FOOD STYLIST: JO

Table of Contents

Introduction

The art of Mexican cooking is a rich and diverse culinary tradition that has been shaped by the country's history and geography. Mexican cuisine is known for its bold and flavorful spices, fresh ingredients, and creative use of traditional cooking techniques. Some of the most popular Mexican dishes include tacos, enchiladas, mole sauce, tamales, and chiles rellenos.

Whether you're a fan of spicy tacos or rich, slow-cooked mole sauce, there's something for everyone to enjoy in this vibrant and delicious culinary tradition.

Chapter 1
Mexican Cooking

The art of Mexican cooking is a celebration of bold flavors, fresh ingredients, and cultural diversity. One of the defining characteristics of Mexican cooking is its use of chili peppers, which are used to add heat and depth of flavor to dishes. Mexican cuisine also relies heavily on herbs and spices, including cumin, coriander, and oregano, to add complexity and aroma to dishes.

In addition to its bold flavors, Mexican cuisine is also known for its cultural and regional diversity. Different regions of Mexico have their own unique cooking styles, ingredients, and dishes, which reflect the history and traditions of the local people. For example, the Yucatán peninsula is known for its use of achiote, a red paste made from annatto seeds, in dishes like cochinita pibil, a slow-roasted pork dish.

Mexican cooking also often features fresh, seasonal ingredients, such as avocados, tomatoes, and corn, which are used in dishes like guacamole, salsa, and elote (Mexican grilled corn). These ingredients not only add flavor and nutrition to dishes, but also reflect the importance of sustainability and local food sources in Mexican cooking.

Why Meat Matters

Meat plays a significant role in Mexican cooking, as it is often used as a key ingredient in many traditional dishes. The use of meat can be traced back to pre-Columbian times, when indigenous peoples raised livestock and hunted wild game for food. Today, meat continues to be an important part of Mexican cuisine, with a variety of different meats used in dishes ranging from tacos to stews.

Some of the most commonly used meats in Mexican cooking include beef, pork, chicken, and lamb. Beef is a staple in many dishes, such as tacos al pastor (spicy marinated pork tacos) and carne asada (grilled beef). Pork is also widely used, especially in dishes like carnitas (slow-cooked, crispy pork) and cochinita pibil (achiote-marinated slow-roasted pork). Chicken is often used in dishes like pollo asado (grilled chicken) and enchiladas, while lamb is used in dishes like barbacoa de borrego (slow-cooked lamb).

In Mexican cooking, meat is typically prepared in a variety of ways, including grilling, roasting, and slow cooking. These cooking methods help to bring out the natural flavors of the meat, while also allowing for the addition of spices and seasonings to create complex and delicious dishes.

Meat is an important part of Mexican cuisine, both for its flavor and for its cultural significance. It is often the centerpiece of meals and is used to create dishes that are both hearty and satisfying. Whether enjoyed as a simple taco or in a complex stew, meat is an essential component of Mexican cooking, and one that continues to play a major role in this rich and flavorful culinary tradition.

RELATIVELY AFFORDABLE CUTS

Mexican cuisine is known for making the most of relatively affordable cuts of meat, such as beef cheek (barbacoa), beef tripe (menudo), and pork shoulder (carnitas). These cuts of meat are often slow-cooked or braised, which helps to tenderize them and bring out their natural flavors. This cooking method also makes these cuts of meat more economical, as they can be stretched further to feed more people.

Mexican cuisine is also known for its use of traditional cooking methods, such as roasting on a spit (al pastor) and slow-cooking in a pit (barbacoa). These methods help to create unique and delicious flavors, and also allow for the use of more affordable cuts of meat that may not be as tender when cooked quickly.

The ingenuity of Mexican cooks in using relatively cheap cuts of meat and traditional cooking methods to create delicious and satisfying dishes has made Mexican cuisine one of the most popular and beloved in the world. Whether you're enjoying a simple taco or a complex mole sauce, Mexican cuisine is a testament to the art of making the most of what you have and transforming it into something truly delicious.

All about Tortillas

WHAT TO LOOK FOR IN A GOOD TORTILLA

A good tortilla is a staple in Mexican cuisine, and there are several key qualities to look for when selecting one. Here are a few things to consider:

Texture: A good tortilla should have a soft and pliable texture, but not be too thick or too thin. It should have a slightly chewy texture, but not be tough or rubbery.

Flavor: A good tortilla should have a mild, slightly toasty flavor, without any off tastes or strong flavors. Corn tortillas should have a slightly sweet, corn-like flavor, while flour tortillas should have a slightly nutty, wheat-like flavor.

Appearance: A good tortilla should have a consistent color and texture, without any tears or holes. Corn tortillas should have a slightly yellow color, while flour tortillas should be a light, creamy white.

Freshness: A good tortilla should be fresh and soft, without any hard or stale spots. If you're buying pre-packaged tortillas, make sure to check the expiration date and look for tortillas that are packaged in a vacuum-sealed bag, which helps to maintain freshness.

Ingredients: A good tortilla should be made with simple, high-quality ingredients, such as corn or flour, water, and a small amount of salt. Avoid tortillas that contain preservatives, artificial flavors, or excessive amounts of oil or fat.

TYPES OF TORTILLAS TO AVOID

There are certain types of tortillas that you may want to avoid, either for health or quality reasons. Here are a few types of tortillas to be cautious of:

Processed tortillas: Some tortillas are highly processed, containing a long list of ingredients and preservatives. These tortillas may have a rubbery texture, a bland flavor, and may not hold up well when used in dishes.

Pre-packaged, shelf-stable tortillas: Some pre-packaged tortillas are designed to have a long shelf life, but this often comes at the cost of quality. These tortillas may have a dry and tough texture, and may contain artificial flavors and preservatives.

Low-quality corn tortillas: Corn tortillas can be an excellent choice when they are made with high-quality corn masa, but low-quality corn tortillas may have a dry and tough texture, and may not have a good corn flavor.

Fried tortilla chips: Tortilla chips are a popular snack food, but many brands are fried in unhealthy oils and contain a high amount of salt and artificial flavors.

It's best to choose tortillas that are made with simple, high-quality ingredients and that are minimally processed. If you're looking for a convenient option, look for tortillas that are packaged in a vacuum-sealed bag, which helps to maintain freshness and quality.

FINDING THE PERFECT TORTILLAS

Some American-made handmade tortillas can be too thick and clumsy. Handmade tortillas can vary greatly in quality, and some may be made with a less traditional recipe that results in a thicker and heavier tortilla.

Thicker tortillas can make it difficult to roll or fold a tortilla, and can overwhelm the fillings in a dish. They may also have a denser texture, making them less tender and less flavorful.

If you're looking for authentic Mexican-style tortillas, it's best to look for tortillas that are made by Mexican or Mexican-American artisans, or that are imported from Mexico. These tortillas are more likely to be made with traditional recipes and techniques, and to have the right balance of flavor, texture, and thickness.

However, it's also important to keep in mind that every cook and every region has its own style and interpretation of a tortilla, so it's always a good idea to try different brands and types to see what you like best.

"YELLOW-ISH" TORTILLAS

Some tortillas can have a dirty-yellow color and a bitter smell due to the addition of too much lime to the cooking water. Lime (also known as calcium hydroxide or "cal") is sometimes added to the cooking water when making corn tortillas to help soften the corn and improve the flavor. However, if too much lime is used, it can result in a bitter taste and a yellowish color that can be unappealing.

In addition to affecting the taste and color of the tortilla, using too much lime can also be harmful to your health, as it can cause gastrointestinal issues and other health problems. To avoid these issues, it's best to look for tortillas that are made with the right amount of lime, or to make your own tortillas using high-quality, fresh masa and a recipe that calls for the appropriate amount of lime.

When selecting a tortilla, look for one that has a consistent color, a tender texture, and a mild, slightly sweet flavor. If you're unsure about the quality of a tortilla, try a small piece before purchasing a larger amount, or ask the vendor or manufacturer for information about the ingredients and production methods used. Tortillas that are too thin, transparent, and chewy, which means that wheat flour has been added to the masa.

BUY FRESH MASA FROM A TORTILLA FACTORY AND MAKE YOUR OWN.

Making your own tortillas using fresh masa can be a fun and rewarding way to experience authentic Mexican cooking. Fresh masa is a dough made from ground corn that has been treated with lime to release the starches and improve the flavor.

To make your own tortillas, simply mix the fresh masa with a little water, salt, and any other seasonings you like, and then shape the dough into small balls. Using a tortilla press or a rolling pin, flatten each ball of dough into a thin, round tortilla. Then, cook the tortillas on a hot griddle or comal until they are golden brown and cooked through.

The process of making your own tortillas may take a little bit of time and practice, but the result will be worth it. Homemade tortillas are fresher, tastier, and more authentic than many store-bought options, and they are also a great way to control the ingredients and seasonings used in your cooking. Whether you're a beginner or an experienced cook, making your own tortillas is a fun and delicious way to experience Mexican cuisine.

OR EVEN A STEP FURTHER......

Making your own nixtamal and having it ground by a tortilla factory to make fresh masa for your tortillas is another great option for authentic Mexican cooking. Nixtamal is a traditional process for treating corn in Mexican cuisine, and it involves soaking dried corn kernels in an alkaline solution of lime and water.

The process of making nixtamal helps to soften the corn and release the nutrients, as well as improve the flavor and texture of the final product. To make your own nixtamal, simply soak the dried corn in the lime and water solution for several hours or overnight, and then rinse and drain the kernels.

Once you have your own nixtamal, you can take it to a tortilla factory or a local tortilla maker to have it ground into fresh masa. The fresh masa can then be used to make your own tortillas, as described above.

Making your own nixtamal and tortillas from scratch can be a time-consuming process, but it is a great way to experience traditional Mexican cooking and to ensure that your tortillas are made with high-quality, authentic ingredients. Whether you're making them for a special occasion or for everyday use, homemade nixtamal and tortillas are sure to be a delicious and satisfying addition to your Mexican cooking.

Chapter 2
Tools and Pantry

Tools

Electric whisk

Using an electric whisk can be very helpful in Mexican cooking, especially when it comes to whipping aquafaba. Aquafaba is the liquid from a can of chickpeas or other beans, and it can be used as a substitute for egg whites in many recipes, including meringue.

An electric whisk can make the process of whipping aquafaba much easier and less tiring than using a handheld whisk, as it does the work for you. The high speed of the electric whisk allows it to quickly whip the aquafaba into a fluffy and stable mixture, similar to meringue. This can be especially useful when making dishes like meringue pies, pavlovas, or whipped toppings, as it saves time and effort and produces a consistent, high-quality result.

If you're interested in using an electric whisk for Mexican cooking or for other culinary purposes, there are many models available on the market, from basic handheld models to stand mixers with a range of attachments. When selecting an electric whisk, consider factors such as power, speed options, and durability to find one that fits your needs and budget. With the right tools, cooking and baking can be a more enjoyable and effortless experience, and you can create delicious and impressive dishes with ease.

HIGH-POWERED BLENDER

A high-powered blender can be very helpful in Mexican cooking. A regular blender may not have enough power to create the smooth and creamy textures required for many Mexican dishes, such as salsas, dips, and sauces. High-powered blenders, on the other hand, are designed to handle tougher ingredients and produce smoother, creamier results.

One of the benefits of a high-powered blender is that it can quickly and efficiently puree ingredients into a smooth consistency, without having to stop and scrape down the sides as often as you would with a regular blender. This can save time and effort and result in a more consistent texture.

In addition, a high-powered blender is less likely to heat up the contents of the blender, This is important because some ingredients, such as avocado or other delicate ingredients, can be affected by heat, which can impact the flavor and texture of the final dish.

Whether you're making salsas, guacamole, or other Mexican dishes, a high-powered blender can be a valuable tool in your kitchen. When selecting a blender, consider factors such as power, speed options, size, and durability to find one that meets your cooking needs and budget. With a high-powered blender, you'll be able to make smooth and creamy Mexican dishes with ease and confidence.

MULTI-COOKER

In traditional Mexican cooking, beans are often used as a staple ingredient in many dishes, including tacos, soups, stews, and salads. Cooking dried beans from scratch can take several hours on the stove, and can be time-consuming and labor-intensive.

With a multi-cooker, such as a pressure cooker or Instant Pot, you can cook dried beans in a fraction of the time. The high pressure and steam generated by the multi-cooker can cook the beans much faster than traditional methods, without sacrificing flavor or texture.

In addition to cooking dried beans, a multi-cooker can also be used for other Mexican dishes, such as stews, soups, and rice. The multi-cooker can be used as a slow cooker or a pressure cooker, depending on the recipe, making it a versatile and convenient tool in your kitchen.

When selecting a multi-cooker, consider factors such as size, capacity, and features, such as sautéing, browning, and slow cooking, to find one that fits your cooking needs and budget. With a multi-cooker, you'll be able to prepare delicious Mexican dishes in a fraction of the time, and enjoy the convenience of one-pot cooking.

SILICONE SPATULA

A silicone spatula can be a very useful tool in Mexican cooking, as well as in any other type of cooking. Silicone is heat-resistant and non-stick, making it ideal for cooking and serving dishes that require a delicate touch.

One of the main advantages of a silicone spatula is its flexible head. The flexible head allows you to easily scrape and mix ingredients in a pan, ensuring that none of the flavorful sauce or juices goes to waste. This is especially helpful when making sauces, salsas, or other dishes that benefit from incorporating every last drop of flavor.

In addition, silicone is also a non-reactive material, which means it won't react with acidic ingredients, such as tomatoes or lime juice, preserving the flavor and color of your dishes. And since silicone is non-stick, it's easy to clean and won't scratch your cookware, making it a long-lasting and practical kitchen tool.

Pantry

FRESH PRODUCE

Some of the most commonly used fresh produce in Mexican cooking include:

Tomatoes: Tomatoes are a staple ingredient in Mexican cooking, used in everything from salsa to soups to sauces.

Onions: White onions are a staple in Mexican cooking and are used raw as a garnish or cooked as a base for sauces and soups.

Garlic: Garlic is used in Mexican cooking for its pungent flavor and aroma. It's used in many dishes, from salsas to stews to sauces.

Cilantro: Cilantro is a popular herb in Mexican cooking, used for its fresh, citrusy flavor. It's used as a garnish, in salsa, and as a flavor component in many dishes.

Jalapeños: Jalapeños are a staple in Mexican cuisine, used for their moderate heat and sweet, earthy flavor. They're used in salsas, stews, and sauces, or served pickled as a condiment.

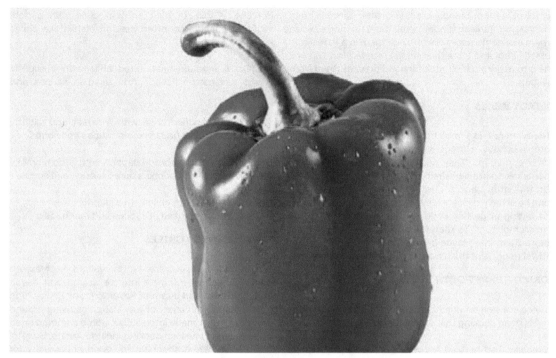

Serranos: Serranos are a popular chile pepper in Mexican cooking, used for their medium heat and bright, grassy flavor. They're used in salsas, stews, and sauces, or served pickled as a condiment.

Poblanos: Poblanos are a mild, slightly sweet chile pepper often used in Mexican cuisine. They're often roasted, peeled, and used in dishes like chiles rellenos.

Avocados: Avocados are a staple in Mexican cuisine, used in everything from guacamole to tacos. They add a rich, creamy texture and nutty flavor to dishes.

Squash: Squash is a staple in Mexican cuisine, used in dishes like soups, stews, and as a filling for tacos and tamales.

ALL ABOUT HERBS

Herbs play an important role in Mexican cuisine, adding flavor, fragrance, and visual interest to dishes. Some of the most commonly used herbs in Mexican cooking include cilantro, epazote, hoja santa, Mexican oregano, and epazote.

Cilantro is often used in salsa, guacamole, and other fresh sauces, as well as in soups, stews, and meats. Its bright, citrusy flavor adds a freshness and brightness to dishes.

Epazote is a pungent herb with a distinctive, earthy flavor. It's often used in beans, soups, and stews, where it helps to reduce the bloating that can occur when eating beans.

Hoja santa is a large, fragrant leaf often used to wrap foods, such as tamales, before they are steamed. The flavor is similar to licorice, anise, and mint.

Mexican oregano has a more robust, slightly bitter flavor than the Mediterranean oregano commonly used in Italian cooking. It's often used in salsas, sauces, and stews, and pairs well with roasted and grilled meats.

By incorporating fresh herbs into your Mexican cooking, you can bring a depth of flavor and aroma to your dishes that is truly representative of Mexican cuisine.

TENDER HERBS

Tender herbs such as cilantro, parsley, and basil are delicate and can easily be damaged by excess moisture. This can cause them to wilt, turn brown, and spoil quickly. To prevent this, it's important to store them properly and to use them as soon as possible after purchasing or harvesting. To keep tender herbs fresh for longer, wrap them in a damp paper towel, place them in a resealable plastic bag, and store them in the refrigerator. This will help to maintain their moisture and prevent them from wilting.

HARDY HERBS

Hardy herbs like rosemary, thyme, bay leaves, and oregano have a tough structure and can withstand drier conditions. They need to be kept in an airtight container to prevent them from drying out completely. On the other hand, tender herbs like cilantro, parsley, and basil have delicate leaves and are more susceptible to wilting or getting soggy if they are exposed to too much moisture. To keep them fresh for a longer time, store them in a plastic bag with a slightly damp paper towel to prevent them from drying out completely.

DRIED HERBS WORTH BUYING

There are several dried herbs that are commonly used in Mexican cooking that are worth buying:

Oregano: This herb adds a warm, earthy flavor to many dishes, including salsas, moles, and stews.

Cumin: This warm and slightly bitter spice is a staple in Mexican cuisine, used to add depth and complexity to dishes like chili, tacos, and refried beans.

Coriander: The seeds of the cilantro plant, coriander has a citrusy, slightly sweet flavor that is used in a variety of Mexican dishes, including salsas, guacamole, and stews.

Cinnamon: This sweet and warm spice is used to add depth and complexity to dishes like hot chocolate, coffee, and sweet breads.

Epazote: This pungent herb is often used in Mexican cooking to add a unique flavor to soups, stews, and bean dishes.

Ancho chili powder: Made from dried ancho chiles, this mild chili powder is used to add depth of flavor and a hint of heat to many Mexican dishes.

ALL ABOUT CHILES

Mexican cuisine uses a wide variety of chiles, both fresh and dried, that can range in heat, flavor, and texture. Here are some of the most commonly used chiles in Mexican cooking:

Jalapeño: A medium-heat chile with a slightly sweet and tangy flavor, often used in salsas, guacamole, and sauces.

Serrano: A hotter chile that is similar in size and shape to a jalapeño, with a slightly more herbaceous flavor.

Poblano: A mild to medium-heat chile with a rich, slightly sweet flavor, often used in dishes like chiles rellenos.

Guajillo: A medium-heat, dried chile with a slightly sweet and earthy flavor, often used in sauces and soups.

Ancho: A mild, dried chile with a sweet and slightly smoky flavor, often used in mole sauces and soups.

Chipotle: A dried, smoked jalapeño with a rich, smoky flavor, often used in adobo sauces, salsas, and soups.

Habanero: A very hot chile with a slightly sweet and fruity flavor, often used in sauces and marinades.

FRESHLY DRIED CHILES

freshly dried chiles are highly valued in Mexican cooking because of their intense aroma and flavor. They add heat and depth of flavor to many dishes, and can be used in a variety of ways, such as being ground into powders or made into sauces. Some common dried chiles used in Mexican cooking include Ancho, Guajillo, and Pasilla. When shopping for dried chiles, look for ones that are soft, pliable, and deeply colored, as these are usually a sign of good quality.

CHILES STORAGE

Store your dried chiles in an airtight container or resealable plastic bag, or extend them further by freezing them in airtight containers or freezer bags. as it helps to preserve their flavor and aroma. By keeping them airtight and away from light, you can prevent oxidation and ensure that they stay fresh for a long time. Freezing is also a great option, as it slows down the process of aging and can keep the dried chiles in good condition for several months. Just be sure to label the containers or bags with the type of chile and the date it was stored, so you know how long it has been frozen and can plan accordingly for your cooking.

Corn and Wheat

Corn is a staple grain in Mexican cooking and is used to make tortillas, tamales, salsas, and other dishes. Corn is also used to make masa, a dough that is the base for many Mexican dishes, including tamales, tortillas, and pupusas.

Wheat, on the other hand, is used in Mexican cooking primarily to make flour tortillas and baked goods like sweet breads, cakes, and empanadas. Some traditional Mexican dishes that use wheat flour include sopapillas, churros, and buñuelos.

Chapter 3
Basics

Chipotle Mayonnaise

Prep time: 5 minutes | Cook time: 8 minutes | Makes 1 CUP / 240G

- 1 egg
- 1 Tbsp freshly squeezed lime juice
- ½ tsp sea salt
- 1 canned chipotle chile in adobo, seeds removed
- ¾ cup / 180ml safflower oil

1. In a food processor or a blender, pulse the egg, lime juice, salt, and chipotle until well combined. With the motor running, add the oil in a slow drizzle, processing until the mayonnaise emulsifies and turns creamy. Partway through, be sure to turn off the processor, scrape the sides, and process again so as not to waste anything. Alternatively, you can do all of this by hand, using a whisk and beating vigorously for about 8 minutes. (In the blender, it should take 4 to 5 minutes.)
2. This mayonnaise is best used on the day you make it, although it can be stored in a sealed container in the refrigerator for up to 2 days.

Strained Fresh Cheese

Prep time: 5 minutes | Cook time: 65 minutes | Makes 2 CUPS / 480G

- 2 cups / 480ml whole milk
- ½ cup / 120ml buttermilk
- ½ cup / 120ml cream
- ¾ tsp sea salt

1. Line your colander with cheesecloth. You want the cheesecloth to drape over the lip of the colander, giving you enough excess to tie up the suspended cheese curds as they drain. Set the colander in the sink.
2. Combine the milk, buttermilk, cream, and salt in a Dutch oven or heavy-bottom stockpot. Place over medium-high heat and stir as the liquid heats up, using a spatula or whisk to keep the forming curds from settling at the bottom of the pot, where they could scorch. As the liquid reaches about 175°F / 80°C, the curds (which look like clumps) and whey will separate, and the curds will rise to the top.
3. Turn off the heat and pour the contents of the pot into the prepared colander. Use a rubber spatula to ease the curds down onto the cheesecloth. You can gently press out the moisture, but don't press hard, since you don't want to mash the curds into the cloth. Tie the four corners of the cloth and suspend the curds over a bowl (I hang the cheesecloth from my sink faucet) to let them drain for at least 30 minutes, or longer, depending on how thick you want the resulting cheese to be. It will have the texture of ricotta after 30 minutes, and if you wait 6 to 8 hours, it will have the consistency of cream cheese.
4. Queso fresco can be stored in a sealed container in the refrigerator for up to 1 week.

Mexican Sour Cream

Prep time: 5 minutes | Cook time: 10 minutes | Makes 2 CUPS / 480G

- 2 cups / 480ml cream
- ¼ cup / 60ml cultured buttermilk

1. In a glass jar, combine the cream and buttermilk. Cover the mouth of the jar with several layers of cheesecloth or a dish towel and let it sit for 24 hours at room temperature (between 70° and 75°F / 20° and 25°C).
2. If your home is chilly (as mine often is in San Francisco), you can set your jar on top of your refrigerator, which tends to be warmer, or in the oven with the oven light on. After 24 hours, screw on the lid of the jar, and refrigerate for 24 hours before using.

Beans Refried In Lard

Prep time: 5 minutes | Cook time: 25 minutes | Serves 4

- 2 cups / 120g drained Soupy Beans
- 1 cup / 240ml reserved bean cooking liquid
- ¼ cup / 50g lard
- ½ tsp sea salt

1. In a bowl, mash the beans to a coarse paste with a potato masher or fork, gradually adding a few tablespoons of the reserved bean cooking liquid periodically as you mash, until you achieve the consistency you want. You don't want any beans left whole, but it's okay if some texture remains. If you prefer very smooth refried beans, you could use a blender or an immersion blender, but I like mine a bit chunky, so I mash mine by hand.
2. Warm the lard in a skillet over medium heat, until it's melted. When you put the tip of a wooden spoon in the hot lard, the wood should sizzle. Add the mashed beans and the salt and then cook, stirring constantly for about 5 minutes. Drizzle in more of the remaining bean cooking liquid if needed to maintain the desired consistency. They should form a thick but creamy paste.
3. The beans can be stored in a sealed container in the refrigerator for up to 5 days. They can also be frozen for up to 6 months, thawed, and reheated in a skillet over low heat.

Corn Tortillas

Prep time: 5 minutes | Cook time: 15 minutes|Makes 12 (6-inch / 15cm) tortillas

- 2 cups / 520g fresh masa
- Water, as needed or 2 cups / 260g masa harina
- 1 to 1¼ cups / 240 to 300ml water

1. If using fresh masa, make sure that it has the consistency of stiff cookie batter. If it doesn't, add water, 1 tsp at a time, until it does.
2. If using masa harina, in a medium bowl, combine the masa harina and 1 cup / 240ml water and mix well. Continue adding water 1 Tbsp at a time until you have formed a smooth and thick dough that has the consistency of stiff cookie dough.
3. Form 12 golf ball–size balls and lay a moist dish towel over them so they don't dry out.
4. Warm an ungreased comal or two skillets over medium heat.
5. Lay a precut sheet of plastic on the bottom of a tortilla press and place a ball of masa on top of the plastic. Place a second sheet of plastic on top of the ball and then squeeze the press firmly so that the dough is sandwiched between the two plates. You want the tortilla to be about ⅛ inch / 3mm thick. Open the press and remove the flattened masa, which will be stuck between the two sheets of plastic. Place it on your left palm (if you're right-handed) and use your right hand to peel off the top sheet of plastic. Then flip it over and transfer it to your right hand, so that it rests in your right palm. Carefully peel off the other sheet of plastic, freeing the raw tortilla.
6. Gently deposit the raw tortilla onto the preheated comal or skillet. You should hear a faint sizzle as it hits the metal. Watch for the edge of the tortilla to begin turning opaque, a signal that it is cooking. When this happens (after 30 to 45 seconds), flip it to the other side and let it cook for 30 to 45 seconds, until the whole thing starts to turn opaque. Now flip it back to the first side and let it cook for a final 30 seconds. After the second flip, it should start to puff up a little, a sign that all of the water in the masa has evaporated and the tortilla is done.
7. Getting your technique down takes some fiddling. If the edges of your tortilla look grainy and dry, add 1 Tbsp water to your dough, massaging it in thoroughly. But don't add too much water, or the masa will stick to the plastic and to the bottom of your pan. Make sure that your tortillas aren't too thinly pressed and that the thickness is uniform, which makes it easier to flip them. You may also need to adjust the heat of your stove if you feel they're cooking too quickly or too slowly. Once you get the moisture and temperature right, each tortilla should take a total of about 2 minutes to cook through. At this point, you should be able to press and cook two tortillas at a time, one on each side of the comal (or in each hot skillet). As each tortilla is finished cooking, set it in a basket or a deep bowl and cover the growing stack with a dish towel to keep them warm as you add to it. Wrapped up well, in a basket or a box with a lid, they should stay warm for about 1 hour.
8. You can reheat a tortilla on a hot comal or in a skillet, flipping it a few times until it's completely heated through. It's okay if your tortilla gets a little charred. The black flecks add flavor. You can also reheat them in a stack. Begin by heating one tortilla. After you flip it, add another on top of the already hot side of the first one. After 30 seconds, flip them both together so that the cold side of the second one is now on the hot surface of the pan, and add a third tortilla to the top of the pile. Keep flipping and adding until you have as many warm tortillas as you need. There's really no limit. Once they're stacked, they will all keep each other warm.

Roasted Peppers

Prep time: 5 minutes | Cook time: 15 minutes|Makes about 7 OZ / 200G

- 4 to 6 large poblano chiles, or as many as you want to roast

1. Remove the charred skin from the whole chiles, trying your best not to puncture them if you intend to stuff them. If you intend to use your roasted chiles for rajas, or strips, then it obviously matters less if the chile tears. If you are careful, you should be able to remove just the thin skin and none of the flesh of the chile.
2. Begin by using the back of a chef's knife to rub away the large pieces. Then use your fingers to pick off the smaller bits. Be thorough, since the lingering bits of blackened skin taste bitter and have a reputation for causing indigestion. Once the chile is thoroughly peeled, use a sharp knife to make a slit from the stem to the tip. Reach inside and, using either your fingers or a knife, remove the veins connecting the seeds to the chile, as well as the seeds. (I don't like to rinse my chiles under water because it removes some of their great flavor.)
3. Store in a sealed container in the refrigerator for up to 1 week.

Harina Flour Tortillas

Prep time: 5 minutes | Cook time: 5 minutes|Makes 12 large (10-inch / 25cm) or 24 small (6-inch / 15cm) tortillas

- 4 cups / 500g all-purpose flour
- 2 tsp baking powder
- 1 tsp sea salt
- ½ cup / 110g lard
- 1½ cups / 360ml hot water

1. In a large bowl, mix the flour, baking powder, and salt.
2. In a small saucepan over low heat, melt the lard, then remove it from the heat.
3. Make a well in the center of your flour mixture and pour the melted lard into it, stirring to incorporate until the mixture has a pebbly texture. Then add the hot water, little by little, stirring and integrating it into the dough, kneading with your hands until it's smooth and stretchy.
4. On a floured countertop, form the dough into a long rope that you can cut into the number of tortillas you want. Depending on the desired size, you should make between 12 and 24 balls. Roll each piece into a ball, then roll them into very thin disks.
5. Line a basket with a dish towel and preheat the oven on the lowest setting (or turn on the oven light).
6. Preheat a large comal or skillet over medium-high heat. You don't need to grease it, since the lard in the dough will keep your tortillas from sticking. Add a tortilla and cook for 30 to 45 seconds, flip it with a metal spatula and cook the other side for another 30 to 45 seconds, until the whole thing starts to turn opaque. Now flip it back to the first side and let it cook for a final 30 seconds. After the second flip, the tortilla should be golden on both sides and starting to puff up a little, a sign that all of the water in the masa has evaporated and the tortilla is done.
7. Put each tortilla in the basket and place in the warm oven until ready to serve.

Red Rice

Prep time: 5 minutes | Cook time: 15 minutes|Serves 4

- ½ cup / 120ml water, plus more as needed
- 4 Roma tomatoes, cored
- ½ white onion, cut into chunks
- 2 Tbsp olive oil
- 1 garlic clove
- 1 sprig cilantro
- 1 cup / 200g long-grain white rice
- 1 tsp sea salt
- ½ cup / 50g fresh or frozen (unthawed) peas (optional)
- ½ cup / 60g minced carrots (optional)

1. In a blender, combine the water, tomatoes, and onion. Blend completely. You need 2 cups / 480ml of liquid to cook the rice, so top off the tomato mixture with more water, as needed.
2. Add the oil to a heavy-bottom saucepan over medium heat until it's hot but not smoking. Add the garlic, cilantro, and rice and fry, stirring constantly, until each grain of rice is opaque.
3. Add the pureed tomato mixture and the salt to the pan. Add the peas and carrots. Bring the mixture to a boil, then decrease the heat to low, return to a simmer, and cover the pot with a lid. Let the rice simmer undisturbed for 15 minutes. Check the rice for doneness by tasting a few grains. They should be tender but not mushy, separate and distinct. If needed, cook for 3 to 5 minutes longer. Remove the garlic and cilantro before serving.
4. While I recommend making this rice right before serving, if you make it ahead of time, empty the cooked rice onto a baking sheet and spread it out until it has cooled; this will keep the rice on the bottom of the pot from overcooking and becoming mushy. Transfer the rice to a sealed container and refrigerate for up to 3 days. You can reheat the rice by steaming it. To do so, place a steamer basket in a pot over gently boiling water, spoon the rice into the basket, place the lid on the pan, and steam for 2 to 3 minutes.

Arroz Rice

Prep time: 5 minutes | Cook time: 10 minutes|Serves 4

- 2 Tbsp olive oil
- 1 garlic clove
- 2 cups / 400g long-grain white rice
- 2 cups / 480ml water
- 1 sprig cilantro
- 1 tsp sea salt, plus more as needed

1. Add the oil to a medium heavy-bottom saucepan. Add the garlic and rice and turn the heat to medium-high. Fry, stirring constantly, until each grain of rice is opaque.
2. Add the water, cilantro, and salt and bring to a boil. Decrease the heat to maintain a simmer, cover the pot with a lid, and cook for 15 minutes without stirring. Check the rice for doneness by tasting a few grains. They should be tender but not mushy, separate and distinct. If needed, cook for 3 to 5 minutes longer. Taste and add more salt if needed. Remove the garlic and cilantro before serving.
3. While cooked rice can be stored in a sealed container in the refrigerator for up to 3 days and reheated, I suggest making it just before you intend to eat it, because it tastes better when freshly cooked.

Green Rice

Prep time: 5 minutes | Cook time: 15 minutes|Serves 4

- 2 cups / 480ml water or chicken stock, plus more as needed
- 1 poblano chile, cut in half lengthwise, stemmed, seeded, and veins removed (or not, depending on how spicy you want this to be)
- ½ cup / 10g cilantro leaves, minced
- 2 Tbsp olive oil
- 1 garlic clove
- ½ white onion, minced
- 1 cup / 200g long-grain white rice
- 1 tsp sea salt, plus more as needed

1. In a small saucepan over high heat, bring the water or chicken stock to a boil, then add the chile and decrease the heat. Let the chile simmer for about 10 minutes until soft. Pour the cooking liquid and the chile into a blender. For a uniformly green rice, add the cilantro and liquefy. For more flecked rice, liquefy only the chile and the liquid and wait to add the cilantro to the cooking pan. You need 2 cups / 240ml of the liquid to cook the rice, but you can top off the green liquid with more water, as needed.
2. Add the oil to a medium heavy-bottom saucepan and warm over medium heat until hot but not smoking. Add the garlic, onion, and rice and fry, stirring constantly, until each grain of rice is opaque.
3. Add the poblano liquid, salt, and the cilantro if not added earlier to the cooking liquid. Bring the

mixture to a boil, then decrease the heat to low; return to a simmer and cover the pot with a lid. Let the rice simmer undisturbed for 15 minutes. Check the rice for doneness by tasting a few grains. They should be tender but not mushy, separate and distinct. If needed, cook for 3 to 5 minutes longer. Taste and add more salt if needed. Remove the garlic before serving.
4. While I recommend making this rice right before serving, if you make it ahead of time, empty the cooked rice onto a baking sheet and spread it out until it has cooled; this will keep the rice on the bottom of the pot from overcooking and becoming mushy. Transfer the rice to a sealed container and refrigerate for up to 3 days. You can reheat the rice by steaming it. To do so, place a steamer basket in a pot over gently boiling water, spoon the rice into the basket, place the lid on the pan, and steam for 2 to 3 minutes.

Refried Beans Refried Beans

Prep time: 5 minutes | Cook time: 25 minutes|Serves 4

- 2 cups / 120g drained Soupy Beans
- 1 cup / 240ml reserved bean cooking liquid
- ¼ cup / 60ml safflower or olive oil
- ½ white onion, minced
- ½ tsp salt

1. In a bowl, mash the beans to a coarse paste with a potato masher or fork, gradually adding a few tablespoons of the reserved bean cooking liquid periodically as you mash, until you achieve the consistency you want. You don't want any beans left whole, but it's okay if some texture remains. If you prefer very smooth refried beans, you could use a blender or an immersion blender, but I like mine a bit chunky, so I mash by hand.
2. Warm the oil in a skillet over medium heat until it's hot but not smoking. Add the onion and cook, stirring until translucent but not browned, about 5 minutes. Add the mashed beans and the salt and then stir constantly for about 5 minutes. Drizzle in more of the remaining bean cooking liquid if needed to maintain the desired consistency. The beans should form a thick but creamy paste. Taste and add more salt if needed.
3. The beans can be stored in a sealed container in the refrigerator for up to 5 days. They can also be frozen for up to 6 months, thawed, and reheated in a skillet over low heat.

Soupy Beans

Prep time: 5 minutes | Cook time: 45 minutes|Serves 4

- 2 cups / 360g dried beans
- 1 garlic clove
- 1 sprig epazote, 1 avocado leaf, or 1 Tbsp dried oregano or marjoram
- Sea salt

1. Rinse the beans thoroughly, removing any debris, then place them in a medium pot and cover with about 4 inches / 10cm of water. In Mexico, we traditionally use a tall clay pot, but any pot will do as long as there's room for the beans to expand as they absorb the cooking water. Add the garlic and the epazote, avocado leaf, oregano, or marjoram.
2. Bring the water to a boil, then immediately decrease the heat to maintain a low simmer and cover the pot with a lid. After 30 minutes, stir the beans, because the ones at the bottom of the pot will cook faster and you want them all done at the same time. Add more water if needed to maintain 2 to 3 inches / 5 to 7.5cm over the top of the beans. Cover and let simmer for another 15 minutes, then taste a bean for doneness. The beans probably will not be finished yet, but at this point, you should start checking them every 10 minutes, stirring gently each time and adding more water if needed. Let the beans cook until they are just a bit softer than you think they should be but still whole, with their skins intact. When you're satisfied that they're well cooked, season with salt.
3. I bring these beans to the table warm, in a bowl of their broth, for people to serve themselves. The beans can be stored in a sealed container in the refrigerator for up to 1 week and gently reheated over low heat, as needed. They can also be frozen for up to 6 months, thawed, and reheated over low heat.

Chicken Stock

Prep time: 5 minutes | Cook time: 55 minutes|Makes about 1 qt / 960ml

- 1 white onion, thinly sliced
- 2 garlic cloves
- 1 fennel bulb, cut in half, or 2 stalks celery
- 2 carrots
- 2 bay leaves (preferably fresh)
- 2 lb / 910g bone-in, skin-on chicken breasts
- About 5 cups / 1.2L water
- 1 tsp sea salt

1. In a large stockpot combine the onion, garlic, fennel, carrots, bay leaves, chicken, water, and salt to a boil over high heat. Decrease the heat and simmer for 20 minutes. Remove the chicken and let it cool. Once you can handle it, tear the meat off the bones and reserve it to use in another dish. Return the bones to the pot and let the stock simmer for an additional 40 minutes.
2. Line a colander with several layers of cheesecloth and set the colander over a bowl. Strain the stock through the colander. Chill the stock if you don't need to use it immediately. Chicken stock will last in a sealed container in the refrigerator for about 5 days, but I use what I need immediately and freeze the rest in containers so that I always have some available.

Fish Stock

Prep time: 5 minutes | Cook time: 55 minutes|Makes about 1 qt / 960ml

- Collars of 2 fish, or the head, bones, and fins of one large fish, or the heads and shells of 1 lb / 455g shrimp
- 3 carrots, cut into small (about 1-inch / 2.5cm) chunks
- 4 stalks celery, cut into chunks
- ½ white onion, cut into chunks
- 1 Roma tomato, cored
- 2 garlic cloves
- 4 bay leaves (preferably fresh)
- 10 black peppercorns
- 2 allspice berries
- 1 chile piquín
- 5 cups / 1.2L water

1. In a large stockpot over high heat, bring the fish bones or shrimp shells, carrots, celery, onion, tomato, garlic, bay leaves, peppercorns, allspice, chile, and water to a boil. Then, decrease the heat and simmer for 45 minutes.
2. Line a colander with several layers of cheesecloth and set the colander over a bowl. Strain the stock through the colander. Chill the stock if you don't need to use it immediately. A seafood stock will last in a sealed container in the refrigerator for about 2 days, but I use what I need immediately and freeze the rest in a container so that I always have some available.

Trejo'S Steak Sauce

Prep time: 5 minutes | Cook time: 55 minutes|Makes about 2 cups

- 1 medium head garlic (about 10 cloves), cloves separated and peeled
- 1 large red onion, roughly diced
- 6 dried guajillo chiles, stems and seeds removed
- ½ cup canola oil
- Juice of 1 lime
- 2 tablespoons agave syrup
- 1 tablespoon adobo sauce from a can of chipotles in adobo (see Trejo's Tip)
- 2 teaspoons kosher salt, plus extra to taste
- 1 teaspoon chipotle chile powder
- 1 teaspoon ground cumin
- 1 teaspoon red wine vinegar

1. Preheat the oven to 350˚F.
2. Spread the garlic cloves and diced onion on an 11 x 17-inch sheet pan and bake until they are golden brown and soft, about 45 minutes. Leaving the oven on, transfer the garlic and onions to a blender.
3. Place the guajillo chiles on the sheet pan and bake them until they are fragrant and lightly toasted, 2 to 5 minutes.
4. Meanwhile, in a medium saucepan, bring 4 cups of water to a low boil. Remove the pan from the heat and let the water cool for 5 minutes.
5. Add the chiles to the water, cover the saucepan, and set it aside for 20 minutes to let the chiles soften.
6. Drain the chiles and roughly chop them. Put them in the blender with the garlic and onions and add the oil, lime juice, agave, adobo sauce, salt, chile powder, cumin, and red wine vinegar. Blend until smooth, then taste and add more salt if needed. Serve immediately or refrigerate in an airtight container for up to 5 days.

Chipotle Crema

Prep time: 5 minutes | Cook time: 5 minutes|Makes about 2 cups

- 2 cups sour cream
- 4 chipotle chiles from a can of chipotle chiles in adobo sauce, plus 2 tablespoons of the adobo sauce
- Juice of 2 limes
- 2 teaspoons kosher salt

1. Put the sour cream, chipotles, adobo sauce, lime juice, and salt in a blender and puree until smooth.
2. Serve immediately or transfer to an airtight container and refrigerate for up to 3 days.

Pepita Pesto

Prep time: 5 minutes | Cook time: 5 minutes|Makes about 1 cup

- About 1½ cups roughly chopped fresh cilantro
- About 2 cups roughly chopped fresh flat-leaf parsley
- 6 garlic cloves
- 1 cup unsalted raw pepitas (pumpkin seeds)
- ½ teaspoon kosher salt, plus extra to taste
- ½ cup pure olive oil

1. Put the cilantro and parsley in a food processor and add the garlic, pepitas, and salt. Pulse for 5 seconds and then scrape down the sides of the bowl. Repeat the pulsing and scraping about 5 more times, until the ingredients are finely minced. While the machine is running, slowly pour the olive oil through the feed tube, processing until the pesto is combined and looks like coarse meal, about 30 seconds, scraping down sides if necessary.
2. Taste and adjust the seasoning with more salt as needed. Use the pesto immediately or transfer it to an airtight container or glass jar and refrigerate it for up to 3 days.

Orange Crema

Prep time: 5 minutes | Cook time: 5 minutes|Makes about 1 cup

- ½ cup sour cream
- ½ cup mayonnaise
- ½ cup orange juice concentrate, thawed

1. In a medium bowl, combine the sour cream, mayonnaise, and orange juice concentrate and mix well to combine.
2. Use immediately or refrigerate in an airtight container for up to 3 days.

Cumin Crema

Prep time: 5 minutes | Cook time: 5 minutes|Makes about 1 cup

- 1 cup sour cream
- 2 tablespoons ground cumin
- 1 teaspoon kosher salt

1. In a small mixing bowl, whisk together the sour cream, cumin, and salt until well combined.
2. Use immediately, or refrigerate in an airtight container for up to 3 days

Creamy Cilantro Lime Vinaigrette

Prep time: 5 minutes | Cook time: 5 minutes|Makes about 2 cups

- 1½ cups chopped fresh cilantro
- ½ cup vegenaise (Just Mayo is good, too)
- Juice of 1 lime

1. For a creamy-smooth dressing, combine the cilantro, vegenaise, lime juice, and ¼ cup of water in a blender and puree until smooth.
2. For a chunkier vinaigrette, combine everything in a medium bowl and whisk until emulsified (that's the fancy word for thoroughly mixed so that the juice is suspended evenly throughout the fats). Use immediately or refrigerate in an airtight container for up to 5 days.

Escabeche Mint Crema

Prep time: 5 minutes | Cook time: 5 minutes|Makes about 1 cup

- 1 cup sour cream
- 2 tablespoons chopped pickled jalapeños or Escabeche
- Juice of 1 lime
- 1 tablespoon roughly chopped fresh mint leaves
- 1 teaspoon ground cumin
- 1 teaspoon kosher salt
- ¼ teaspoon cayenne pepper

1. Put the sour cream, jalapeño, lime juice, mint, cumin, salt, and cayenne in a blender and puree until smooth.
2. Serve immediately or transfer to an airtight container and refrigerate for up to 3 days.

Lime Crema

Prep time: 5 minutes | Cook time: 5 minutes|Makes about 1 cup

- 1 cup sour cream
- 1 teaspoon finely chopped lime zest
- Juice of 1 lime
- 1 teaspoon kosher salt

1. In a small mixing bowl, combine the sour cream, lime zest, lime juice, and salt and mix well. Serve immediately or refrigerate in an airtight container for up to 3 days.

Vegan Cashew Crema

Prep time: 5 minutes | Cook time: about 3 hours|Makes about 2 cups

- 2 cups raw unsalted cashews
- Juice of 1 lime, plus extra to taste
- Juice of 1 lemon, plus extra to taste
- 1½ teaspoons kosher salt, plus extra to taste

1. Place the cashews in a blender jar and cover them with 1½ cups of water. Set the cashews aside to soak for at least 2 hours or up to overnight. The longer they soak, the softer they'll get, making for a creamier result.
2. Pour off the water and add the lime juice, lemon juice, and salt to the cashews. Puree until creamy and smooth. Taste and adjust with more salt, lemon, and/or lime juice if needed. Use immediately or refrigerate in an airtight container for up to 5 days.

Avocado Crema

Prep time: 5 minutes | Cook time: 5 minutes|Makes about 2 cups

- 2 medium avocados, halved, pitted, and peeled
- ½ cup sour cream
- ½ cup roughly chopped fresh cilantro
- Juice of 1 lime, plus extra to taste
- 1 teaspoon kosher salt, plus extra to taste

1. Combine the avocados, sour cream, cilantro, lime juice, and salt in a blender and puree until smooth.
2. Taste and add more salt or lime juice if desired. Use immediately or store in an airtight container for up to 3 days.

Purple Sweet Potato Ice Cream
Prep time: 5 minutes | Cook time: 15 minutes| Serves 4

- 2 large purple sweet potatoes
- 1 (14-oz [414-ml]) can full-fat coconut milk, refrigerated
- ½–¾ cup (120–180 ml) pure maple syrup
- 1 tbsp (15 ml) vanilla
- 1 tbsp (8 g) tapioca flour
- 1½ cups (360 ml) unsweetened coconut milk
- Pinch of salt
- Edible flowers, to garnish (optional)

1. Preheat the oven to 400°F (200°C).
2. Place the sweet potatoes on a baking sheet, and poke holes in them using a fork. Cover with foil and roast for about 1 hour until soft and tender. Allow the sweet potatoes to cool completely.
3. Add 1½ cups (300 g) of peeled sweet potato to a blender. Open the can of coconut milk and scoop out all the fat on the surface and any solid pieces floating in the coconut milk, and add to the blender. Add ½ cup (120 ml) of the maple syrup, vanilla, tapioca flour, unsweetened coconut milk and salt. Blend until smooth and creamy. Taste and add more maple syrup if needed. Add the ice cream base to a medium plastic container with a lid so the base is 2 to 3 inches (5 to 8 cm) high and place in the freezer for at least 3 hours.
4. Once the ice cream is set, you can use an ice cream scoop to make round ice-cream balls. Top with edible flowers, if desired.

Fresh Papaya with Raspberry Yogurt
Prep time: 5 minutes | Cook time: 5 minutes| Serves 2

- 1 papaya, halved and seeded
- 1¼ cups (225 g) low-fat raspberry frozen yogurt, softened
- ½ cup (75 g) frozen raspberries
- 1 tablespoon sugar

1. Fill the papaya halves with the frozen yogurt, then place in the freezer overnight.
2. In a blender or food processor, puree the raspberries and sugar. Strain to remove seeds, if desired. Transfer to a covered container and refrigerate until ready to serve.
3. Just before serving, remove the papaya from the freezer. Remove the skin and transfer each papaya half to a plate. Drizzle with the raspberry sauce and serve immediately.

Figs with Cheese
Prep time: 5 minutes | Cook time: 35 minutes| Serves 4

- For the Cream Cheese
- 1 cup (145 g) raw cashew pieces
- ¼ cup (60 ml) water, plus extra if needed
- 2–3 acidophilus probiotic capsules
- 1 tsp lemon juice, plus extra if needed
- Salt, to taste
- For the Candied Pepitas
- 2 tbsp (30 ml) maple syrup
- 2 tbsp (28 g) raw sugar
- Pinch of salt
- 1 cup (138 g) pepitas
- For the Figs
- 8 medium figs
- ¼ cup (60 ml) pure maple syrup, divided

1. To make the cream cheese, soak the cashews for 3 hours or overnight. Add the soaked and drained cashew pieces to a blender with the water, and blend until completely smooth. Scrape down the sides of the blender with a spatula to get any bits that didn't blend, and add more water if necessary to create a thick and creamy consistency. Once smooth, add the probiotic powder from the capsules and discard the casings. Pulse to incorporate the probiotic powder.
2. Use a spatula to scrape the cream out of the blender and into a glass bowl. Cover the bowl with a cheesecloth, mesh bag or plastic wrap with holes poked into the surface. Allow the mixture to sit at room temperature and ferment for 15 to 18 hours, or until it is tangy and cheesy. Add the lemon juice and salt to the mixture and mix until fully incorporated. Taste for salt and lemon juice and add more as needed. Set aside.
3. To make the candied pepitas, preheat oven to 375°F (190°C).
4. Add the maple syrup, sugar and salt to a medium saucepan and heat over medium heat. Stir constantly until the sugar is melted and the mixture is slightly foamy.
5. Add the pepitas and stir until they are fully coated. Lightly coat a medium baking sheet with oil, and spread the pepitas on the sheet. Bake for 10 minutes, stirring them halfway through. Remove the seeds from the oven and let them cool completely. You can stir the seeds occasionally while cooling to prevent them from sticking to the pan.
6. For the figs, preheat the oven broiler on high. Cut off the fig stems and make an X cut in the top of each fig until you get about halfway through each fig. Place the figs on a small baking sheet and drizzle them with 2 tablespoons (30 ml) of the maple syrup. Add them to the top oven rack, and broil for about 5 to 10 minutes, or until they look soft, slightly charred and release their juices. Take the figs out of the oven, and allow them to cool slightly until they are warm. Use 2 small spoons to add the cream cheese to the center of each fig. Drizzle them with the remaining maple syrup and garnish with the candied pepitas.

Avocado Ice Cream

Prep time: 5 minutes | Cook time: 15 minutes| Serves 4

- For the Ice Cream
- 2 medium Hass avocados
- ⅓ cup (80 ml) pure maple syrup
- 1 tbsp (15 ml) vanilla
- ½ cup (120 ml) unsweetened almond milk
- Pinch of salt
- 6 tbsp (90 ml) melted refined coconut oil
- For the Chocolate Ganache
- 3 tbsp (21 g) raw cacao powder
- 3 tbsp (45 ml) melted refined coconut oil
- 3 tbsp (45 ml) pure maple syrup
- 1 tsp vanilla
- For Serving
- ¼ cup (36 g) microplaned pistachios

1. To make the ice cream base, add the avocados, maple syrup, vanilla, almond milk and salt to a blender. Blend until smooth and creamy. Put the blender on low speed, and slowly pour in the coconut oil so it is evenly incorporated into the mixture.
2. Add the ice cream base to a medium plastic container with a lid so the ice cream base is 2 to 3 inches (5 to 8 cm) high and place in the freezer for at least 3 hours.
3. To make the ganache, add the cacao, melted coconut oil, maple syrup and vanilla to a small bowl and whisk until completely smooth. If it hardens, place it over the stove or on a double boiler to loosen it up. Once the ice cream is set, you can use an ice-cream scoop to make round ice-cream balls. Use a spoon to pour the melted ganache over the ice cream. Top with pistachio shavings.

Watermelon Agua Fresca

Prep time: 5 minutes | Cook time: 5 minutes| Makes 6 cups

- 4 cups (600 g) cubed seedless watermelon
- ¼ cup (60 ml) fresh lime juice
- 2 tablespoons superfine sugar (optional)
- Lime slices

1. Place the watermelon, lime juice, 4 cups (960 ml) water, and the sugar, if using, in a blender and blend well. Strain through a fine-mesh strainer.
2. Refrigerate for 1 hour or until well chilled. Serve in a glass filled with ice and garnish with a slice of lime.

Tropical Fruit Mold

Prep time: 5 minutes | Cook time: 65 minutes| Serves 8

- Two 0.3-ounce (8.5 g) packages sugar-free orange-flavored gelatin
- 2 cups (480 ml) boiling water
- 1½ cups (360 ml) guava nectar
- 1 mango, peeled, pitted, and diced

1. Dissolve the gelatin in the boiling water in a medium bowl. Add the guava nectar and stir to combine. Pour into dessert glasses or bowls and refrigerate until slightly thickened, 45 to 60 minutes.
2. Stir in the mango and refrigerate until firm, about 3 hours. Serve cold.

Piña Colada Pie

Prep time: 5 minutes | Cook time: 5 minutes| Serves 8

- 3¼ cups (245 g) light whipped topping
- 1¾ cups (455 g) low-fat coconut-flavored Greek yogurt, preferably "toasted coconut vanilla"
- 1 cup (195 g) drained canned crushed pineapple
- 1 store-bought graham cracker pie crust

1. Mix together the whipped topping, yogurt, and pineapple in a large bowl. Spoon the mixture into the crust.
2. Cover tightly and freeze overnight. Allow to soften slightly before serving.

Chocolate Bread Pudding

Prep time: 5 minutes | Cook time: 55 minutes| Serves 6

- 3 wheat bolillo or birote (day-old bread) chopped into ½-inch (1.3-cm) dice
- 6 cups (1.4 L) unsweetened almond milk
- ½ cup (43 g) raw cacao powder
- 1 (7-oz [198-g]) piloncillo raw sugar cone
- 2 whole Mexican cinnamon sticks
- 3 whole cloves
- 2 bananas, divided
- 1 Gala apple, cored and quartered
- 1 tbsp (14 g) vegan butter (optional)
- ¼ cup (42 g) raisins
- ¼ cup (29 g) sliced almonds
- ¼ cup (16 g) shredded unsweetened toasted coconut

1. Turn the oven broiler on high. Layer the bread cubes on a baking sheet and place under the broiler for 1 to 2 minutes, or until the bread is toasted throughout. Remove from the oven and set aside to cool.
2. Pour the almond milk and cacao powder in a medium pot over medium heat. Whisk to fully incorporate the cacao. Add the piloncillo, cinnamon, cloves, 1 whole peeled banana and the apple. Bring to a boil, and then turn down to a simmer. Stir until the piloncillo has dissolved. Let it steep for 15 minutes with the heat off. Strain and pour the liquid back into the pot.
3. Grease a baking dish with vegan butter (if using). Line the bottom of the dish with a layer of the toasted bread. Pour ¼ of the liquid over the bread and cover with banana slices from the remaining banana and ⅓ of the raisins, almonds and coconut. Add another layer of bread and repeat the process. You should be able to fit 2 to 3 layers of bread. When the final layer of bread has been laid out, pour the remaining liquid on top and cover with the remaining raisins, almonds and coconut. Cover with aluminum foil and allow the capirotada to set in the refrigerator for at least 2 to 3 hours or overnight so the bread fully absorbs most of the liquid prior to baking.
4. Preheat the oven to 350°F (180°C). Allow the capirotada to come back to room temperature. Bake for 30 minutes, remove the foil, and bake for an additional 5 minutes to brown and crisp the top. Remove from the oven and let it rest for 20 minutes before serving.

Mangoes and Strawberries With Cream

Prep time: 5 minutes | Cook time: 5 minutes| Serves 4

- 1 cup (245 g) low-fat vanilla yogurt
- 1 tablespoon brown sugar, or to taste
- 2 teaspoons almond extract
- 2 large mangoes
- 4 large strawberries
- ¼ cup (25 g) slivered almonds, toasted
- Mint leaves (optional)

1. Mix together the yogurt, sugar, and almond extract in a small bowl until smooth. Divide evenly among four plates, forming a circle on each plate.
2. Peel and pit the mangoes, then cut each lengthwise into eight slices. Arrange four slices in a sunburst pattern on each plate.
3. In a blender or food processor, puree the strawberries. Pour the strawberry puree in the center of the plates with the mangoes. Garnish with the almonds and mint leaves, if desired.

Mango Mold

Prep time: 5 minutes | Cook time: 10 minutes| Serves 8

- Two 0.3-ounce (8.5 g) packages sugar-free orange-flavored gelatin
- One 0.3-ounce (8.5 g) package sugar-free lemon-flavored gelatin
- 1 cup (240 ml) boiling water
- 8 ounces (227 g) neufchatel cream cheese, cubed
- 1 cup (165 g) diced mango
- Mango slices, strawberries, and/or raspberries (optional)

1. Pour the gelatin and boiling water into a blender. Remove the blender lid's center insert, place a clean kitchen towel over the blender opening, and blend until the gelatin dissolves. Add the cream cheese and diced mango and blend until smooth.
2. Pour into a mold or other container and refrigerate until set, about 3 hours. Garnish with mango slices, if desired, before serving.

Chapter 6
Soups and Stews

White Beans with Battered Salted Cod

Prep time: 5 minutes| Cook time: 65 minutes| Serves 8

- About 3 pounds (1.4 kg) salted cod fillets, without bone, cut into 2 x 4-inch strips
- 2¼ pounds (1 kg) navy beans, drained
- 1 tablespoon plus 1½ cups (360 ml) vegetable oil
- ½ cup (50 g) finely chopped white onion
- 4 cloves garlic, 2 cloves roughly chopped and 2 cloves minced
- 2¾ cups (500 g) chopped tomatoes
- 4 whole cloves
- 4 whole allspice berries
- 1 teaspoon cumin seeds
- 1 cup (40 g) minced fresh cilantro
- 1 sprig of fresh epazote
- 1 cup (120 g) all-purpose flour
- 8 egg whites plus 6 egg yolks
- Sea salt, if needed
- Corn tortillas (store-bought or homemade)

1. Rinse the salted cod under running water and rub off as much of the salt as you can with your fingertips.
2. Fill a large container or mixing bowl with water, add the fish, cover, and let soak overnight to remove as much salt as possible. After a night of soaking, the fish should have softened slightly.
3. In a large heavy-bottomed pot, combine the beans and 5 quarts (4.7 L) of water. Bring to a boil, cover, and lower the heat to a simmer. Cook until tender, about 45 minutes to an hour. Once cooked, pour the beans through a colander and discard the cooking water. In the same heavy-bottomed pot, heat the 1 tablespoon vegetable oil in a large skillet over medium heat. Add the onion, roughly chopped garlic, and tomatoes and cook until the tomatoes change color to a lighter red, about 5 minutes. Add the beans, stir well, and let cook for another 5 minutes. Add 8 cups (2 L) of water back to the pot and bring to a low simmer while you make the next steps. Season lightly with about 1 teaspoon of salt, keeping in mind that the fish is salted.
4. Meanwhile, in a molcajete, grind the minced garlic, cloves, allspice, and cumin seeds until finely ground. Add this paste to the soup, along with the cilantro. Keep simmering for another 10 minutes.
5. In another large heavy-bottomed pot, bring 4½ cups (1 L) of water and the epazote to a boil. Lower to a slow simmer, add the pieces of fish and cook for 2 minutes. Remove and place on a plate. Pat dry with a paper towel.
6. Place the flour on a wide plate and lightly dredge each piece of fish on both sides.
7. In a large mixing bowl, beat the egg whites until medium-stiff peaks form. Add the egg yolks and mix well. Using a pair of tongs, dip each piece of floured fish into the beaten eggs. Shake excess batter from the fish.
8. Pour the 1½ cups (360 ml) oil into a large skillet and bring to frying temperature. When hot, using tongs, carefully drop each piece of fish into the oil and fry for about 2 minutes on each side, until both sides are golden brown. When done, remove to a paper towel–lined plate to drain excess oil.
9. Bring the simmering beans to a boil. Once boiling, gently add the fried pieces of cod into the pot of beans. Continue boiling the beans with fish for 2 minutes. Taste for seasonings and add salt if necessary (remember that the fish is already salty).
10. To serve, ladle stew into bowls and serve with tortillas.

Pork Feet in Black Beans

Prep time: 5 minutes| Cook time: 45 minutes| Serves 6

- 2 pounds (910 grams) pork feet (ask the butcher to cut them in quarters; should be 4 pieces)
- 2 tablespoons white vinegar
- 2 pounds (910 grams) black beans, rinsed
- 1 medium onion (100 grams), quartered
- 4 cloves garlic (20 grams)
- 1½ tablespoons of sea salt, plus more to taste
- 10 epazote leaves
- For The Toppings
- Sliced pickled jalapeños and their pickling liquid
- Minced onion
- Lime wedges

1. Put the pork feet in a bowl with enough water to cover. Add the vinegar and let soak for 5 minutes. Rinse.
2. In a heavy-bottomed pot, bring 3 quarts (3 L) of water to a boil. Add the beans, pork feet, onion, and garlic. When it starts to boil, reduce the heat to low and simmer, covered, for about 30 minutes. (If the water evaporates along the way, add hot water to cover.)
3. Add the epazote and salt to taste. Continue cooking until the pork feet are soft and the beans are tender and cooked through, about 40 minutes or more.
4. Serve in bowls and offer sliced jalapeños and their pickling liquid, minced onion, and lime wedges as toppings.

Oaxacan Chicken Soup

Prep time: 5 minutes| Cook time: 55 minutes| Serves 4 To 6

- 3 tablespoons sea salt
- 1 whole chicken (about 2 pounds/1 kg), butchered into eight pieces
- ½ small white onion (50 g), quartered, plus ½ cup chopped white onion (50 g)
- 1 slice (90 g) white bread
- ½ teaspoon cumin seeds
- ⅛ teaspoon black peppercorns
- 3 whole cloves
- 1 tablespoon dried oregano
- 1 tablespoon vegetable oil
- 3 cloves garlic, minced
- 1⅔ cups (300 g) chopped tomatoes
- 3 serrano chiles, stems removed
- For The Garnishes
- 4 to 6 limes, sliced
- 2 tablespoons chunky sea salt
- White rice
- Warm tortillas

1. In a large, heavy-bottomed pot, bring 10½ cups (2.5 L) of water to a boil and add the salt. Put the chicken and onion half in the pot. Lower the heat to a simmer and cook, covered, for 40 minutes. Once the chicken is cooked, remove it from the broth and set aside. Remove and discard the onion.
2. In a medium-sized mixing bowl, combine the bread and 1 cup (60 ml) of the chicken broth. Once the bread has soaked up all the broth, put the bread in a blender with another ½ cup (60 ml) of broth and puree.
3. In a molcajete or spice grinder, grind the cumin seeds, peppercorns, cloves, and oregano until finely ground.
4. Heat the oil in a large skillet over medium heat. When hot, add the chopped onion, garlic, spices and oregano, and tomatoes. Stir and cook for 8 minutes or until the tomatoes start to change color.
5. Put the tomato mixture, chicken, serrano chiles, and pureed bread in the pot of broth. Bring the chicken soup back to a simmer and continue to simmer for 10 minutes more or until the chiles change color.
6. Serve with sliced lime, a chunky salt, white rice, and tortillas.

Chicken in Green Salsa with Potatoes and Cactus

Prep time: 5 minutes| Cook time: 35 minutes| Serves 4 To 6

- 1 whole chicken (about 2 pounds/1 kg), butchered into eight pieces
- Sea salt and freshly ground black pepper
- 3 tablespoons vegetable oil
- 1 cup (170 g) peeled and halved baby potatoes
- Generous 1 pound (500 g) tomatillos (preferably the purple Milpero variety), husked and rinsed
- ¼ cup (35 g) chopped white onion
- 3 cloves garlic, minced
- 1 serrano chile, stem removed
- 1 cup (40 g) chopped cilantro
- 3½ ounces (100 g) nopales, dethorned and sliced into 1-inch (2.5 cm) strips
- 1 cup (240 ml) chicken broth
- Corn tortillas (store-bought or homemade), for serving

1. Generously season the chicken pieces with salt and pepper.
2. Heat the oil in a Dutch oven or other heavy-bottomed pot over medium heat. When hot, add the chicken pieces and brown them for about 5 minutes on each side until a very light golden coating forms. Lower the heat. Add the potatoes and cook for another 5 minutes, lightly stirring so the potatoes get a little brown as well.
3. Meanwhile, in a blender, combine the tomatillos, onion, garlic, serrano chile, and cilantro with 1 cup (240 ml) of water and blend until smooth.
4. Carefully add this raw salsa and the chicken broth to the pot. Raise the heat and bring to a boil, stirring occasionally. Bring back down to a simmer and cook for 20 minutes or until the chicken is cooked through. Taste for salt and adjust as necessary. Add the nopales and simmer for 5 minutes more. Serve with tortillas.

Cow Foot Soup

Prep time: 5 minutes| Cook time: 35 minutes| Serves 4 To 6

FOR THE BEEF

- 2 tablespoons sea salt
- 2½ pounds (1.2 kg) cow foot, sliced by your butcher
- 1 small white onion, cut into wedges
- ½ head of garlic (about 6 cloves), plus 5 cloves (15 g), peeled
- 6 guajillo chiles (30 g), stems removed
- ½ cup (75 g) tomatillos, husked and rinsed
- 4 whole cloves, freshly ground
- 1 teaspoon freshly ground cumin seeds
- ¼ teaspoon freshly ground black peppercorns
- For The Garnishes
- Corn tortillas (store-bought or homemade), for serving
- Minced fresh cilantro
- Minced onion
- Lime wedges

MAKE THE BEEF

1. In a large heavy-bottomed pot, bring 3 generous quarts (2.8 L) of water to a boil and add the salt, cow foot, half the onion, and the ½ head of garlic. Lower to a simmer and cook, covered, for 4 to 6 hours. Skim any impurities that rise to the top of the broth. When the cow foot is the texture of gelatin and falling apart, turn off the heat. Remove any onion and garlic that hasn't broken down into the broth.
2. Meanwhile, in a 2-quart (2 L) saucepan, bring 2 cups (480 ml) of water to a boil. Turn off the heat, add the chiles, and let soak for 30 minutes or until the chiles have softened. Drain.
3. In a blender, combine the tomatillos, chiles, onion, garlic, and ground spices. Blend until smooth. Pass through a double-fine-mesh strainer and add the puree to the broth. Bring the soup up to a simmer and continue simmer for 10 minutes more.
4. Taste for salt and adjust as necessary. Serve with tortillas and fresh cilantro, onion, and lime wedges for garnish.

Refried Black Beans

Prep time: 5 minutes | Cook time: 35 minutes| Serves 4

- ¼ cup pure olive oil
- ½ medium yellow onion, diced
- 4 to 5 large garlic cloves, chopped
- 1 medium jalapeño, chopped
- 4 cups canned black beans, drained, liquid reserved
- 2 teaspoons ground cumin
- 1 teaspoon kosher salt
- ¼ teaspoon cayenne pepper

1. Heat a cast-iron skillet over medium-low heat for 2 minutes and then add the olive oil. Add the onion, garlic, and jalapeño and cook until the vegetables are soft but not browned, stirring them occasionally, about 10 minutes.
2. Add the beans, cumin, salt, and cayenne. Smash the beans with a large fork or a potato masher until you have a mixture of textures: not too chunky, not too smooth.
3. Cook, stirring occasionally, until the mixture is sweetly fragrant and has thickened slightly, about 10 minutes. Taste the beans to check if they're tender. If not, stir in ¼ cup of the reserved bean liquid and cook 5 minutes more and taste again. Add bean liquid until the desired consistency is reached (we make our beans so they are a little thicker than soup; if you run out of bean liquid, add water). Serve immediately or refrigerate in an airtight container for up to 3 days.

Squash Vine in a Green Mole Soup with Crispy Masa Dumplings

Prep time: 5 minutes| Cook time: 20 minutes| Serves 6

- For The Chochoyotes
- ¼ teaspoon sea salt
- 8¾ ounces (250 g) fresh masa quebrajada
- 1 teaspoon plus 2 tablespoons vegetable oil
- For The Soup
- 8 cups (800 g) guias (squash vines), woody stems removed, leaves reserved, or substitute with fresh spinach
- 3½ cups (400 g) chopped summer squash
- 2 teaspoons sea salt
- 10½ ounces (300 g) fresh masa
- ½ teaspoon cumin seeds
- ½ cup (50 g) white onion
- 4 cloves garlic, peeled
- 1 serrano chile, stem removed
- ¼ cup (40 g) tomatillos, preferably the purple Milperos variety, husked and rinsed
- ⅓ cup (60 g) chopped green tomato

MAKE THE CHOCHOYOTES

1. In a glass measuring cup, dissolve the salt in 3 tablespoons of water. In a mixing bowl, combine the broken masa, salted water, and 1 teaspoon of the oil. Mix until the ingredients turn into a paste.
2. Using your hands, assemble small balls weighing about 10 grams each (about the size of a cherry tomato). You should have enough masa to make around 24 balls. Use your thumb to press down on each ball to create an imprint.
3. Heat the remaining 2 tablespoons of oil in a skillet over medium heat to just below the smoking point. Working in two batches, fry chochoyotes until golden brown on both sides, about 2 to 3 minutes per side. Remove each one to a paper towel–lined plate and reserve.

MAKE THE SOUP

4. Separate the squash vine leaves and stems in different containers. In a large heavy-bottomed pot, bring 8 cups (2 L) of water to a boil. Add the squash and cook for 5 minutes. Add the guia stems and the salt. If using spinach, add spinach with leaves and stems attached all at once and cook for 5 minutes. Lower the heat to a simmer while you prepare the masa slurry.
5. In a blender, combine the masa and 2 cups (120 ml) of water. Blend until smooth and pass through a double-fine-mesh strainer. Pour the masa slurry into the simmering pot of squash. Bring back up to a boil. When boiling, add the squash leaves. Lower the heat to a simmer and continue to cook for about 7 minutes while you prepare the salsa base.
6. Heat a comal or dry skillet over medium heat and toast the poleo (if using) and the cumin for 2 minutes or until fragrant. Grind the spices in a molcajete or spice grinder until finely ground.
7. In the blender, combine the onion, garlic, chile,

tomatillos, tomato, and ½ cup (120 ml) of water and blend until smooth. Add the toasted, ground spices and blend until evenly incorporated. Add the vegetable mixture to the simmering pot and simmer for 8 minutes more. Add salt, about 1 teaspoon or more. Taste and adjust seasonings if needed.
8. Serve the soup in bowls with crispy chochoyotes placed on top.

Beef Soup with Guajillo Chile

Prep time: 5 minutes| Cook time: 1 hour 35 minutes| Serves 4 To 6

- 2 tablespoons sea salt
- 2 pounds (910 g) bone-in short ribs, sliced by your butcher
- 2 pounds (910 g) beef shank, sliced by your butcher
- 2¼ cups (300 g) chopped carrots
- 4 cups (600 g) sliced potatoes
- 2 cups (220 g) sliced chayote
- 2 cups (220 g) trimmed green beans
- 4⅓ cups (400 g) sliced cabbage
- 5 guajillo chiles (25 g), seeds and stems removed
- 1 small white onion (100 g), quartered
- 3 cloves garlic, peeled
- 1 teaspoon freshly ground cumin seeds
- ¼ teaspoon freshly ground black peppercorns
- 2 whole cloves, freshly ground
- ½ cup (75 g) tomatillos, husked and rinsed
- ½ cup (20 g) fresh cilantro
- 1 sprig of fresh mint
- For The Garnishes
- Minced onion
- Minced serrano or jalapeño chiles
- Lime slices

1. In a large, heavy-bottomed pot, bring 1 gallon (3.8 L) of water to a boil and add the salt, short ribs, and beef shank. Lower the heat to a simmer and cook, covered, for 90 minutes. Skim any impurities that rise to the top of the broth.
2. Add the carrots, potatoes, and chayote to the pot. Simmer for 20 minutes. Add the green beans and cabbage. Continue to simmer for 20 minutes while you rehydrate the chiles.
3. Bring the 2 cups (240 ml) of water to a boil in a small pot. Turn off the heat then add the chiles and soak to rehydrate them.
4. After 10 minutes, put the softened chiles in a blender along with the onion, garlic, spices, and tomatillos. Blend until smooth. Strain through a double-fine-mesh strainer and add the puree to the simmering broth. Simmer for 5 minutes, then add the cilantro and mint. Turn off the heat and let the soup sit for 10 minutes. Serve with onion, chiles, and lime.

Beef Stew with Sweet Green Peppers

Prep time: 5 minutes | Cook time: 35 minutes | Serves 8

- 4 tablespoons rendered lard or extra-virgin olive oil, divided
- 1 medium white onion (10 oz/300 g), chopped
- 1 medium green bell pepper (6.34 oz/180 g), stemmed, seeded, and chopped
- 2 large chiles x'catik/güeros/caribes, banana, or cubanelle (5.07 oz/144 g), stemmed, seeded, and chopped
- 6 garlic cloves, finely grated
- 2¼ pounds (1 kg) beef shanks, oxtails, or neck bones
- 1 tablespoon plus 1 teaspoon Morton kosher salt (0.9 oz/28 g)
- 1 teaspoon freshly ground black pepper
- 2 ears corn, shucked and cut into 2-inch lengths
- 2 large green plantains (24 oz/680 g), peeled and cut into ½-inch-thick rounds
- 1 pound (453 g) winter or summer squash, cut into rounds
- 1 large Yukon Gold potato (9 oz/255 g), peeled and cut into 1-inch pieces
- 1 medium sweet potato, preferably purple (9 oz/255 g), peeled and cut into 1-inch pieces
- 1 medium chayote (6.6 oz/188 g), peeled, seeded, and cut into 1-inch pieces
- 2 large Roma tomatoes (6.27 oz/178 g), cored and chopped
- 8 ounces (226 g) malanga or taro root, peeled and cut into 1-inch pieces
- 8 ounces (226 g) yuca, peeled and cut into 1-inch pieces
- 8 ounces (226 g) green beans, trimmed and cut into 3-inch pieces
- ¼ cup chopped fresh cilantro (1.41 oz/40 g)
- ¼ cup chopped fresh flat-leaf parsley (1.41 oz/40 g)

1. In a large heavy pot over medium-high, heat 2 tablespoons of the lard. Add the onion, bell pepper, x'catik, and garlic and cook, stirring occasionally, until beginning to brown, for 8 to 10 minutes. Transfer to a bowl; set aside. In the same pot, heat the remaining 2 tablespoons lard and cook the beef, turning occasionally, until browned on all sides, for about 4 minutes per side.
2. Add the salt, black pepper, and 8 cups water and bring to a boil. Cover the pot, reduce the heat to medium-low, and simmer for 1½ hours. Add the reserved onion mixture, corn, plantains, squash, potatoes, chayote, tomatoes, malanga, and yuca. Cover and cook, stirring occasionally, until the beef is very tender and easily comes off the bone, for about 1 hour. Add the beans. Cover the pot and cook until the beans are crisp-tender, for about 5 minutes. Remove the pot from the heat and let the soup sit for 10 minutes.
3. Divide among bowls. Top with the cilantro and parsley. Serve with warm tostadas.

Creamy Chicken Stew with Oregano

Prep time: 5 minutes | Cook time: 1 hour 25 minutes | Serves 6 TO 8

- ½ cup (2.2 oz/63 g) pepitas/raw pumpkin seeds, plus more for serving
- 4 tablespoons rendered lard, olive oil, or vegetable oil, divided
- 8 large fresh yellow chiles güeros/caribes, banana, or cubanelle (1¼ lb/564 g), halved and seeded, stems on, divided
- 1 large white onion (14 oz/400 g), cut into thin wedges, divided
- 1 medium green bell pepper (6.34 oz/180 g), stemmed, seeded, and quartered
- 6 garlic cloves, lightly crushed
- 3¾ teaspoons Morton kosher salt (0.9 oz/26 g), plus more to taste
- 1 small bunch of fresh cilantro (1.76 oz/50 g)
- 3 fresh oregano or marjoram sprigs
- 1 tablespoon coriander seeds
- 1 teaspoon black peppercorns
- 1 whole chicken (3½ lb/1.5 kg), cut into 10 pieces
- 2 large Roma tomatoes (6.25 oz/178 g), cored and quartered
- 1.1 pounds (500 g) fresh white fine-grind corn masa for tortillas

1. Heat a large skillet over medium-high heat. Toast ½ cup of the pepitas, tossing, until fragrant and browned in spots, for 3 to 4 minutes. Transfer to a bowl.
2. In a large heavy pot over medium, heat 2 tablespoons of the lard. Cook half of the chiles güeros, half of the onion, and all of the bell pepper, garlic, and salt, stirring, until tender but not taking on any color (if they start to brown, reduce the heat), for 8 to 10 minutes. Add the cilantro, oregano, coriander seeds, and peppercorns; cook, stirring constantly, until very fragrant, for about 2 minutes. Add the chicken and 12 cups water. Bring to a boil, reduce the heat to medium-low, and simmer, uncovered, until the chicken is cooked through and pulls easily away from the bone, for 40 to 50 minutes.
3. Meanwhile, arrange a rack in the center of the oven and preheat to 425°F.
4. On a large sheet pan, spread the tomatoes and remaining chiles güeros and onion. Drizzle with the remaining 2 tablespoons lard. Roast, tossing the chiles once or twice, until browned, for 15 to 25 minutes. Season with salt; let cool.
5. Transfer the chicken to a plate. Strain the stock through a fine-mesh sieve set over a large bowl (discard the solids). Transfer 4 cups of the stock to a blender and add the masa and toasted pepitas. Puree until smooth.
6. Wipe out the pot. Pour in the masa mixture and the remaining stock and bring to a simmer. Season with salt and add the chicken to warm through.
7. Divide the stew among bowls. Top with the chiles, onion, tomatoes, and pepitas.

Pozole Mixteco

Prep time: 5 minutes| Cook time: 55 minutes| Serves 12

- For The Mole
- 2 cups (480 ml) vegetable oil
- 3 ancho chiles (50 g), stems removed
- 6 pasilla chiles (50 g), stems removed
- 10 guajillo chiles (50 g), seeds and stems removed
- 7 mulato chiles (50 g), seeds and stems removed
- 10 chiles de arból (10 g), seeds and stems removed
- 8 costeño chiles (10 g), seeds and stems removed
- ¼ cup (35 g) whole raw almonds
- ¾ cup (100 g) diced white onion
- ⅔ cup (100 g) garlic cloves, peeled
- 1 ripe plantain (about 250 g), peeled and sliced
- 1¼ cups (215 g) chopped tomatoes
- 6 ounces (170 g) tomatillos, husked and rinsed
- 1⅓ cups (145 g) sliced apples
- ⅓ cup (50 g) seedless raisins
- 1 tablespoon dried oregano
- ½ cinnamon stick
- Sea salt

MAKE THE MOLE

1. Heat ½ cup (120 ml) of the oil in a large skillet over medium heat. When the oil is hot, fry all of the chiles in batches, about 1 minute each batch. The chiles should be brown and crispy but not burnt. Set them aside and discard the oil.
2. In the same pan over medium heat, heat another ½ cup (120 ml) of oil and fry the almonds until they puff up, 5 to 7 minutes. Remove the almonds and set them aside. (All of the ingredients, separate from the fried chiles, can be piled on top of each other after frying.) In the same oil, sauté the onion until translucent, about 5 minutes. Remove and set aside. Repeat this process with the garlic cloves, plantain, tomatoes, tomatillos, apples, and raisins. Add the oregano and cinnamon stick to the pile of fried items.
3. In a blender, working in batches, blend half of the chiles with 2 cups (480 ml) of water until smooth. Remove and set aside. Add the other half of the chiles with another 2 cups (480 ml) of water and blend until smooth. Remove and set aside.
4. In the same blender, combine the fried almonds, onion, garlic, plantains, tomatoes, tomatillos, apples, raisins, cinnamon, and oregano with 1 cup (120 ml) of water. Blend until pureed and smooth. Depending on your blender, you may need to add more water to make sure that the texture is smooth and uniform.
5. Once you have your pile of blended chile paste and your pile of the rest of the blended ingredients, heat 1 cup (120 ml) of the oil in a large pot over medium heat and wait until it gets hot. Drop in all of the chile paste and stir for 8 minutes until the paste starts to change to a darker color. Remove from the heat and set aside.
6. After the chile paste changes color, add the blended fried mixture to the pot of cooked chile paste. Over medium heat, mix until the rest of the ingredients are mixed in with the chile paste. Taste for salt and season accordingly. Lower the heat and mix and mix until the mole is reduced by half. This should take about 1 hour and the bottom of the pot should be visible. Keep mixing and mixing. It will all be worth it. The final texture should resemble a pasty hummus.

FOR THE BROTH

7. 4½ pounds (2 kg) cooked hominy, drained and rinsed
8. Sea salt
9. 2 pounds (910 g) pork spine, sliced by your butcher
10. 2 pounds (910 g) pork knuckle, sliced by your butcher
11. 1¾ pounds (800 g) pork leg, sliced by your butcher
12. 1 cup (125 g) chopped white onion
13. ¼ cup (35 g) garlic cloves, peeled
14. 6 fresh hoja santa leaves (you can substitute with dried)

FOR THE GARNISHES

15. Minced raw onion
16. Lime slices

MAKE THE BROTH

17. In a large stockpot over high heat, bring 8 quarts (7.5 L) of water to a boil. Once boiling, add the hominy. Lower the heat to medium and simmer for 45 minutes. Taste for seasoning and add salt accordingly.
18. Add all the meat. Keep simmering. After 30 minutes, skim all impurities that rise to the top, then drop in the onion and garlic. Boil for another 45 minutes.
19. Once the meat starts to become tender, about an hour later, add the hoja santa, and season with salt. Cover the pot and lower the heat to a slow simmer. Leave at a simmer for another hour. Once the meat is starting to fall apart, the pozole is ready.
20. Serve with minced raw onion and lime slices, adding the mole paste to your pozole to your liking.

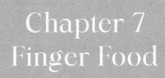

Chapter 7
Finger Food

Roasted Pumpkin Seeds with Chile and Lime

Prep time: 5 minutes | Cook time: 25 minutes | MAKES 2 CUPS / 280G

- 4 chiles de árbol, stemmed and seeded
- 2 cups / 240g pumpkin seeds
- 1 lime, cut in half
- 1 tsp sea salt

1. Preheat the oven to 350°F / 180°C.
2. Warm a medium skillet over low heat. Place the chiles in the skillet and let them toast for 1 to 2 minutes while agitating them. As soon as you can smell the chiles, add the pumpkin seeds to the skillet and move them around constantly as they toast for another 3 to 4 minutes. Pumpkin seeds burn easily, so you want to monitor them closely and keep them from sticking to the pan. Once you can smell a nice toasted aroma (not the smell of burnt seeds), remove the pan from the heat and empty the pumpkin seeds and chiles into a bowl. Remove and discard the chiles. Squeeze the lime juice over the seeds, toss, sprinkle with the salt, and toss again.
3. Coat a baking sheet with oil or use a sheet of parchment paper to keep the seeds from sticking. Spread the seeds evenly on the prepared baking sheet and bake for 10 to 15 minutes, using a spatula to turn them over after the first 5 minutes. You are looking for the seeds to dry out, but they shouldn't turn much darker.
4. Serve the seeds while they're still warm. Theoretically, these seeds can be stored in a sealed container for up to 1 week—if you have any left.

Summer Squash and Asparagus Salad

Prep time: 5 minutes | Cook time: 15 minutes | Serves 6

- 5 or 6 young zucchini or yellow squash or a mix, sliced into ribbons ⅛ inch / 3mm thick
- 1 bunch of asparagus, fibrous base of each stalk trimmed off and discarded, sliced crosswise into ⅛-inch / 3mm-wide pieces
- 1 tsp sea salt, plus more as needed
- 3 Tbsp / 45ml extra-virgin olive oil
- ¼ cup / 60ml freshly squeezed lime juice
- 1 serrano chile, stemmed, seeded, veins removed (or not, depending on how spicy you want this to be), and finely diced

1. Place the zucchini and/or squash and asparagus in a colander, toss with the salt, and leave it in the sink to drain for 5 to 10 minutes. Don't leave it for much longer or the squash will get too limp.
2. In a bowl, whisk together the oil, lime juice, and chile. Add the squash and asparagus slices and toss gently to coat. Taste and add more salt if needed.
3. Serve on individual salad plates or in shallow bowls.

Cactus, Avocado, Tomato, and Summer Squash Salad

Prep time: 5 minutes | Cook time: 15 minutes | Serves 6

- 1 cactus paddle, dethorned
- 3 tsp sea salt, plus more as needed
- 5 or 6 baby squash, preferably yellow and green and differently shaped, sliced about ⅛ inch / 3mm thick
- 4 Roma tomatoes, cored and cut in half
- ½ white onion
- 2 or 3 serrano chiles, stemmed, seeded, and veins removed (or not, depending on how spicy you want this to be)
- ¼ cup / 60ml extra-virgin olive oil
- ¼ cup / 60ml freshly squeezed lime juice
- 1 avocado, cut in half, pitted, peeled, and thinly sliced
- ¼ cup / 5g cilantro leaves, minced, or cilantro flowers if available
- 4 radishes, thinly sliced on a mandoline and placed in a bowl of ice water to curl

1. Place the cactus paddle in a bowl, sprinkle both sides with 1 tsp salt, and set aside for 1 hour. Transfer the cactus to a colander and rinse them thoroughly until they no longer feel slimy. Cut the cacti into ¼-inch / 6mm-wide strips and transfer to a large salad bowl.
2. Place the squash in a colander, add 1 tsp salt, and leave it in the sink to drain for about 10 minutes while you assemble the rest of the salad. Don't leave it for much longer or the squash will get too limp.
3. Meanwhile, in a food processor, combine the tomatoes, onion, chiles, and the remaining 1 tsp salt and pulse until minced but still chunky. You don't want to liquefy these ingredients, because you will be straining the pico de gallo to use only the juices, and the liquid that strains out should be clear, not pink, which it will become if you blend it too thoroughly. Suspend a fine-mesh strainer over a bowl and pour the contents of the food processor into the strainer, catching the juices in the bowl. Remember that you are keeping the juices that strain out, not discarding them.
4. Being careful not to crush or break the sliced squash, gently press out the excess moisture and transfer the squash to the large bowl with the cactus. Don't rinse the squash, since the leftover salt will season the salad. Add 3 Tbsp / 45ml of the oil and the lime juice and toss gently to coat. Taste and add more salt if needed.
5. Serve on individual salad plates or in shallow bowls. Divide the vegetables evenly. Top each portion of squash and cactus with a few slices of avocado. Ladle with the pico de gallo broth and drizzle with the remaining 1 Tbsp oil. Garnish with the cilantro or cilantro flowers and a few slices of radish before serving.

Octopus Salad

Prep time: 5 minutes | Cook time: 25 minutes| Serves 6

- 4 Yukon gold potatoes
- 2 Tbsp sea salt
- 1 cooked octopus, chopped into ½-inch / 12mm pieces
- 1 large fennel bulb, diced
- ½ cup / 10g parsley leaves, chopped
- ⅔ cup / 160ml extra-virgin olive oil
- Juice of 2 lemons
- Maldon sea salt or another finishing salt

1. In a medium saucepan, cover the potatoes with water, leaving their skins on to preserve the starch. Add the salt and bring to a boil. Decrease the heat and let them simmer for 15 to 20 minutes. Test the potatoes with a fork for doneness; they should be soft but not falling apart. Transfer to a colander to drain. Remove their skins (they should slip right off) and let the potatoes cool until you can handle them. Cut the potatoes into ½-inch / 12mm cubes.
2. Place the potatoes in a serving bowl and add the octopus, fennel, and parsley. Dress with the oil and lemon juice. Taste and add the finishing salt if more salt is needed. Since the potatoes and octopus were both cooked in salted water, you may not need additional salt.
3. Store the salad in the fridge until you're ready to serve; use the same day it is made.

Roasted Corn In Its Own Broth

Prep time: 5 minutes | Cook time: 15 minutes| Serves 6

- 6 ears white corn, shucked
- 1 Tbsp sea salt, plus more as needed
- ¼ cup / 5g coarsely chopped epazote or cilantro
- 3 chiles piquín
- 1 recipe freshly made Chipotle Mayonnaise
- Grated queso Cotija or ricotta salata for serving
- 2 limes, cut into quarters
- Ground chile piquín for serving

1. Place a comal or skillet over high heat and oil it lightly so that the corn doesn't stick. Place the ears of corn on the comal or skillet and rotate every 30 seconds or so, until they are lightly charred on all sides, 4 to 5 minutes total. Let the corn cool to the touch, then slice off the kernels.
2. Place the kernels in a medium saucepan over medium-high heat and add water to barely cover, then add the salt, epazote, and chiles. Bring to a boil, then decrease the heat and let simmer for 5 minutes. You have to make sure that the corn is cooked through but not overcooked to the point of being mushy. It should be soft enough to chew easily while still retaining a slight crunch. Remove the chiles. Divide the kernels and liquid evenly among serving bowls and serve warm, passing the mayonnaise, cheese, limes, and ground chile

for people to add if they wish.
3. Esquites can be stored in a sealed container, covered, in the refrigerator for 2 to 3 days. Reheat in a saucepan over low heat.

Green Salad with Pumpkin Seed Dressing

Prep time: 5 minutes | Cook time: 5 minutes| Serves 6

- 1 serrano chile, stemmed, seeded, and veins removed (or not, depending on how spicy you want this to be)
- 1 small garlic clove, toasted lightly in a dry skillet over low heat
- ½ cup / 60g raw pumpkin seeds
- 1 Tbsp flat-leaf parsley leaves
- 2 Tbsp freshly squeezed lime juice
- ½ cup / 120ml extra-virgin olive oil
- ½ tsp sea salt, plus more as needed
- 4 to 6 cups / 80 to 120g of the best, freshest lettuce you can find

1. In a food processor, blend the chile, garlic, pumpkin seeds, parsley, lime juice, oil, and salt. Set aside.
2. Wash and dry the lettuce well, being careful not to crush or bruise the leaves. Toss with the dressing in a large bowl, taste, and add more salt if needed. Serve immediately.
3. Any leftover dressing can be stored in a sealed container in the refrigerator for up to 1 week.

Cactus and Purslane Salad with Ricotta Salata

Prep time: 5 minutes | Cook time: 15 minutes| Serves 6

- 1 lb / 455g cactus paddles, dethorned
- ½ cup / 130g sea salt
- 3½ oz / 100g radishes, sliced on a mandoline
- ½ red onion, slivered
- 6 cups / 120g purslane, rinsed, dried, and torn into manageable bites
- 2 Tbsp chopped cilantro leaves
- ½ cup / 120ml extra-virgin olive oil
- ½ cup / 120ml freshly squeezed lime juice
- 1 tsp Maldon sea salt or another finishing salt
- 4 to 6 Tbsp / 20 to 30g grated ricotta salata

1. Place the cactus paddles in a bowl, sprinkle with the sea salt, and let rest for 1 hour. Transfer the paddles to a colander and rinse them thoroughly until they no longer feel slimy. Cut them into ½-inch / 12mm-wide slices and transfer to a medium serving bowl.
2. Add the radishes, onion, purslane, and cilantro to the bowl. In a jar or a small bowl, combine the oil, lime juice, and finishing salt and shake or stir to mix. Dress the salad and toss to coat.
3. Serve within 1 hour of dressing the salad, topping each portion with 1 Tbsp ricotta salata right before you serve it.

Spicy Crab Soup

Prep time: 5 minutes | Cook time: 15 minutes| Serves 6

- 6 lb / 3kg fresh Dungeness or other crab, cut in half and well cleaned
- 4 bay leaves (preferably fresh)
- 1 cinnamon stick
- ¼ cup / 65g sea salt, plus 2 tsp
- 2 chiles de árbol, stemmed and seeded
- 2 guajillo chiles, stemmed and seeded
- ¼ white onion
- 1 garlic clove
- 12 black peppercorns, or ½ tsp freshly ground black pepper
- 4 Roma tomatoes, cored
- 1 tsp dried oregano
- 1 tsp ground cinnamon
- 4½ cups / 1L plus 65ml water
- 2 Tbsp olive oil
- 2 sprigs epazote
- 1 lime, cut into quarters
- 1 avocado, cut in half, pitted, peeled, and sliced
- ¼ cup / 5g cilantro leaves, minced
- Tortilla chips for serving

1. Start by making sure that your crab is well cleaned, so that all of the innards have been removed. Place the crabs in a large heavy-bottom stockpot and cover them with water. Add the bay leaves, cinnamon, and ¼ cup / 65g salt. You may notice that this is a lot of salt; when you boil crab, you want the water to be as salty as the ocean. The salt will permeate the meat and give it good flavor. Bring to a boil over high heat, then decrease to low and simmer. Cover the pot and let the crabs cook for 15 minutes, until the shells turn bright red. Using tongs, remove the crabs from the pot, place in a colander, and rinse immediately under cold water. If you skip this step, the crabs will continue to cook after leaving the pot and could become tough.
2. Warm an ungreased comal or skillet over medium heat. Begin by toasting only the chiles de árbol, since they have thinner skin than the guajillos and will be finished more quickly. As they toast, stir constantly or rotate with tongs for 1 to 2 minutes and remove them from the heat as soon as they start to smell nutty, before they brown or blister. Set them aside while you toast the guajillo chiles, onion, garlic, and peppercorns, agitating them as you did the chiles de árbol, for 2 to 3 minutes. Remove the guajillos from the heat once they look lightly browned and you can smell their toasted fragrance but before they smell burnt. Remove the stems of the chiles.
3. In the jar of a blender, combine the toasted chiles de árbol and guajillo chiles mixture, tomatoes, remaining 2 tsp salt, ground black pepper, oregano, cinnamon, and ½ cup / 120ml water and liquefy.
4. Over medium heat, in a 4- to 6-qt / 960ml to 1.4L Dutch oven or large heavy-bottom stockpot, warm the oil. When the oil is shimmering, pour in the contents of the blender and fry this sauce for 1 to 2 minutes, until the red color deepens. Add the remaining 4 cups / 960ml water and the epazote, bring to a boil over high heat, then decrease to low and simmer while you remove your crabmeat from the shells. Add all of the meat back to the pot and cook for 1 minute more—just long enough to heat the crab through. Remove the epazote and discard.
5. Divide the chilpachole into soup bowls to serve. Bring the lime, avocado, and cilantro to the table for people to help themselves. A bowl of fresh tortilla chips also makes a nice accompaniment, to scoop up the large chunks of crabmeat from the bottom of your bowl.

Potato Leek Soup

Prep time: 5 minutes | Cook time: 10 minutes| Serves 6

- 1 garlic clove
- 4 Roma tomatoes, cored and quartered
- 5 cups / 1.2L vegetable stock (if making a vegetarian version)
- 1 Tbsp sea salt, plus more as needed
- 1 Tbsp olive oil
- 2 large leeks, cut in half lengthwise, thoroughly washed, and white parts only cut into ⅛-inch / 3mm-thick slices
- 2 potatoes, peeled and diced or cut into thin sticks
- Leaves of a few sprigs oregano or thyme

1. In the jar of a blender, combine the garlic, tomatoes, stock, and salt and blend to liquefy.
2. In a large Dutch oven or heavy-bottom stockpot, warm the oil over medium-high heat until it's shimmering. Add the leeks and fry until translucent, 3 to 4 minutes. Add the contents of the blender and the potatoes and bring to a boil. Decrease the heat and simmer for about 10 minutes, or until the potatoes are soft. Taste and add more salt if needed. Garnish with the oregano or thyme and serve.
3. This soup can be stored in a sealed container in the refrigerator for up to 1 week.

Squash Blossom Soup

Prep time: 5 minutes | Cook time: 25 minutes| Serves 6

- 2 Tbsp butter
- 1 leek, white parts only, thoroughly washed and sliced into fine rings
- 2 qt / 2L water
- 2 Tbsp sea salt
- 3 sprigs epazote or oregano
- 1 garlic clove
- Kernels from 2 ears of white corn
- 2 small zucchini, finely chopped or sliced on a mandoline
- 1 big bunch of squash blossoms, stems and sepals removed, coarsely chopped

1. In a medium to large Dutch oven or heavy-bottom stockpot melt the butter over medium-high heat until shimmering but not smoking. Add the leek and fry for 3 to 4 minutes, until light gold, stirring to keep it from sticking and browning too much. Add the water and the salt, 2 sprigs of the epazote or oregano, and the garlic. Bring to a boil, then decrease the heat to low and simmer for 15 minutes to reduce. Add the corn and cook for 2 minutes, then add the zucchini and cook for an additional 2 to 3 minutes. Remove and discard the garlic. Toss in the squash blossoms and immediately turn off the stove.
2. Mince the remaining sprig of epazote or the leaves of the remaining sprig of oregano.
3. Ladle the soup into serving bowls and sprinkle with the herbs to add a nice perfume to the soup. Serve the soup immediately, since the flowers look and taste best right after they're cooked.

Cold Avocado Soup

Prep time: 5 minutes | Cook time: 25 minutes| Serves 6

- 3 avocados, cut in half, pitted, and peeled
- 6 oz / 170g soft goat cheese
- 2 cups / 480ml Chicken Stock
- ½ cup / 10g cilantro leaves
- 1 serrano chile, stemmed, seeded, veins removed (or not, depending on how spicy you want this to be), and minced
- 1 tsp sea salt
- Healthy pinch of freshly ground black pepper
- Ricotta salata for serving

1. In the jar of a blender, liquefy the avocados, goat cheese, stock, cilantro, chile, salt, and pepper. Chill for 20 minutes before serving.
2. Ladle the soup into bowls. Crumble the ricotta salata over the top of the bowls and serve.
3. If you have soup left over, add a squeeze of lime to prevent it from turning brown. It can be stored in a sealed container in the refrigerator for 1 to 2 days. Rewhip it in the blender before serving.

Avocado Stuffed with Shrimp

Prep time: 5 minutes | Cook time: 35 minutes| Serves 6

- 2 or 3 avocados, cut in half and pitted
- ¼ head napa cabbage or 2 heads Little Gem lettuce (you want something crunchy), finely chopped
- 1 fennel bulb, cut into ¼-inch / 6mm dice
- 2 radishes, cut into ¼-inch / 6mm dice
- ¼ white onion, cut into ¼-inch / 6mm dice
- 5 oz / 140g cherry tomatoes, diced
- 1 lb 6 oz / 630g cooked bay shrimp, well drained
- 3 Tbsp / 45g Mayonesa con Limón
- Juice of 1 lemon, plus more as needed
- 1 tsp sea salt, plus more as needed
- Leaves of 2 or 3 sprigs cilantro, minced

1. Use a large spoon to carefully scoop the flesh of each halved avocado out of its shell, setting the intact avocado halves on a serving platter or, if you intend to serve them individually, on salad plates.
2. In a medium bowl, combine the cabbage or lettuce with the fennel, radishes, onion, and tomato. Add the shrimp, mayonnaise, lemon juice, and salt and toss. Taste and add more salt or lemon juice as needed.
3. Serve a generous scoop of shrimp salad in each avocado half. It's fine if it spills over—no one will complain! Garnish each serving with a sprinkle of pumpkin seeds and fresh oregano or thyme leaves. Eat within 30 minutes, before the avocado begins to turn brown.

Shrimp Broth

Prep time: 5 minutes | Cook time: 15 minutes | Serves 6

- 2 guajillo chiles, stemmed and seeded
- 2 ancho chiles, stemmed and seeded
- 2 cascabel chiles, stemmed and seeded
- 1 Roma tomato, cored
- 1 garlic clove
- 1 cup / 240ml water
- 2 qt / 2L Fish Stock
- 1¾ oz / 50g dried shrimp
- 2 sprigs epazote
- 2 tsp sea salt, plus more as needed
- 12 to 18 raw medium shrimp, peeled, deveined, cleaned, and cut in half or into bite-size pieces
- ½ white onion, minced
- ½ cup / 10g cilantro leaves, chopped
- 2 serrano chiles, stemmed, seeded, veins removed (or not, depending on how spicy you want this to be), and finely minced
- 2 limes, quartered
- 1 avocado, cut in half, pitted, peeled, and thinly sliced

1. On an ungreased comal or in a skillet over medium-high heat, lightly toast the guajillo, ancho, and cascabel chiles, stirring them constantly or turning them with tongs, until they have released their scent but are not dark or blistered. Add them to a blender jar together with the tomato, garlic, and water and liquefy. Empty the contents of the blender into a medium to large Dutch oven or heavy-bottom stockpot and turn the heat to low.
2. In the jar of the blender, combine the stock and dried shrimp and liquefy. Pour this mixture into the pot with the blended chiles. Add the epazote and salt and bring to a boil. Decrease the heat to low and simmer for about 10 minutes, until reduced and thickened. Taste and add more salt if needed. Add the raw shrimp and cook for 3 to 4 minutes, just until they turn pink.
3. Ladle the soup into bowls and serve immediately, passing the onion, cilantro, serranos, limes, and avocado at the table for guests to help themselves.
4. This soup can be stored in a sealed container in the refrigerator for 2 to 3 days.

Zihuatanejo-Style Ceviche

Prep time: 5 minutes | Cook time: 15 minutes | Serves 6

- 1 lb / 455g very fresh firm-fleshed fish, such as halibut or mahi-mahi, filleted and cut into thin (about ½-inch / 12mm) slices
- 1 small red onion, slivered
- 2 serrano chiles, stemmed, seeded, veins removed (or not, depending on how spicy you want this to be), and cut into slivers
- 1 cup / 240ml freshly squeezed lime juice
- 2 tsp sea salt, plus more as needed

1. In a medium bowl, combine the fish, onion, chiles, lime juice, and salt. Stir to coat and then set in the refrigerator to chill for 10 to 15 minutes before serving. (Less time and it will still be raw, but more time and it will start to become tough.) Before serving, taste to check that you like the texture and to see if it needs any more salt.
2. You can store ceviche overnight in the refrigerator, but the lime will thoroughly "cook" the raw fish, and ceviche starts oxidizing after a day. Ceviche is tastiest the day it is made, so don't make more than you intend to serve and eat.

Mushroom Soup

Prep time: 5 minutes | Cook time: 15 minutes | Serves 6

- ¼ cup / 60ml olive oil
- 1 cup / 200g finely sliced green onions, white parts only
- 1 chile de árbol
- 1 tsp sea salt, plus more as needed
- 2 garlic cloves, minced
- 8½ oz / 240g mushrooms, diced
- Chiffonade of 8 to 10 epazote leaves
- 1 qt / 960ml vegetable stock (if making a vegetarian version)
- Chiffonade of 4 or 5 squash blossoms (optional)

1. In a medium to large Dutch oven or heavy-bottom stockpot, warm the oil over medium-high heat until shimmering but not smoking. Drop in the chile and fry for 30 seconds. Add the green onions and ½ tsp of the salt and cook until the onion is translucent but not browned. Add the garlic and sauté for 1 to 2 minutes more, just until you can smell it. Add the mushrooms, epazote, and remaining ½ tsp salt. Salting in stages like this allows the different flavors to come out, and salting the mushrooms separately encourages them to release their tasty juices.
2. Let the mushrooms cook down for about 5 minutes, until they are translucent. Then add the stock and bring to a boil. Immediately decrease the heat and let simmer gently for 10 minutes. Taste and add more salt if needed.
3. Remove the chile and stir in the squash blossoms. Some people prefer to serve a whole squash blossom on top of each bowl of soup, which is pretty but is more for looks than taste.
4. This soup can be stored in a sealed container in the refrigerator for up to 4 days.

Green Soup with Fish Meatballs

Prep time: 5 minutes | Cook time: 45 minutes| Serves 6

- 1 recipe Fish Stock, made using 2 lb / 910g cod or another white-fleshed fish
- 1 bunch of cilantro, rinsed well
- 1 bunch of parsley, finely chopped
- 4 garlic cloves
- 2 serrano chiles, stemmed, seeded, and veins removed (or not, depending on how spicy you want this to be)
- 2 tsp sea salt, plus more as needed
- 2 new potatoes, cut into ½-inch / 1cm cubes
- 4 eggs
- 1 cup natural puffed rice cereal
- Pinch of freshly ground black pepper
- 1 cup / 140g all-purpose flour
- Lime wedges for serving

1. In a large Dutch oven or heavy-bottom stockpot over high heat, bring the stock to a boil. As soon as the stock comes to a boil, decrease the heat to low and simmer for about 30 minutes. Carefully strain out the fish and vegetables; discard the vegetables and set the fish aside to cool until you can handle it.
2. Place the strained stock in the jar of a blender. You will have about 2 qt / 2L. Add all of the cilantro, half of the parsley, the garlic, chiles, and 1 tsp of the salt and liquefy.
3. Pour the contents of the blender into the pot and add the potatoes, which will thicken the soup. Place the pot over low heat and, as the soup simmers, make your fish balls.
4. Break 3 of the eggs into a bowl and whisk. Once the fish is completely cool, pick out any small bones and flake the fish into the eggs. Add the remaining parsley, cereal, remaining 1 tsp salt, and pepper and mix well. With your hands, pat the mixture into golf ball–sized rounds. Break the remaining egg into a separate small bowl and beat well. Spread the flour on a plate. Roll each fish ball first through the beaten egg and then through the flour.
5. Drop the fish balls into the simmering broth and let them cook for 8 to 10 minutes, until firm and cooked through. Taste the soup and add more salt if needed. Serve immediately, with a squeeze of lime.
6. This soup can be stored in a sealed container in the refrigerator for 2 to 3 days. To reheat, bring to a simmer in a saucepan over low heat.

Yucatecan Lime Soup

Prep time: 5 minutes | Cook time: 25 minutes| Serves 6

- ½ cup / 120ml olive oil
- 1 cup / 140g diced white onion
- 1 garlic clove, minced
- 3 or 4 Roma tomatoes, diced
- 2 qt / 2L Chicken Stock
- 1 sprig epazote or hoja santa leaf
- 1 tsp sea salt, plus more as needed
- 2 large chicken breasts
- ½ cup / 120ml safflower oil
- 6 Corn Tortillas, cut into skinny strips
- Juice of ½ orange
- Zest and juice of 1 lime

1. In a Dutch oven or heavy-bottom stockpot over medium heat, warm the olive oil until it's shimmering but not smoking. Add the onion and garlic and cook until the onion is translucent but not browned. Add the tomatoes and bring to a boil. Pour the stock into the pot and add the epazote or hoja santa and salt. Return to a boil and add the chicken breasts, then decrease the heat and simmer for 15 to 20 minutes until the chicken is completely cooked.
2. While the chicken is poaching in the broth, line a plate with a brown paper bag.
3. Once the chicken is poached, remove it from the stock and set it aside until it's cool enough to handle. Remove and discard the epazote or hoja santa. Add the orange juice, lime zest, and lime juice to the soup. Taste and add more salt if needed, depending on how salty your broth was.
4. Ladle the broth into serving bowls. Shred the chicken and divide it among the bowls. Top with the fried tortilla strips and serve hot.
5. This soup can be stored in a sealed container in the refrigerator for 2 to 3 days. To reheat, bring to a simmer in a saucepan over low heat.

Shrimp Cocktail

Prep time: 5 minutes | Cook time: 5 minutes| Serves 6

- 1 cup / 240ml tomato juice
- 1 Tbsp fish sauce
- 1 Tbsp Valentina Salsa Picante
- 1 Tbsp Búfalo Salsa Clásica (typical Mexico hot sauce from the 1960s)
- ½ cup / 115g ketchup
- ½ cup / 120ml freshly squeezed orange juice
- 3 Tbsp / 45ml freshly squeezed lime juice
- 1 lb / 455g cooked bay shrimp
- ¾ cup / 100g chopped white onion
- ¾ cup / 120g diced tomatoes (use whatever is lovely: cherry tomatoes, heirloom, Roma)
- ½ cup / 10g cilantro leaves, chopped
- Sea salt
- 1 avocado, cut in half, pitted, peeled, and cubed

1. In a medium bowl, combine the tomato juice, fish sauce, Valentina and Búfalo hot sauces, ketchup, orange juice, and lime juice. Add the shrimp, onion, tomatoes, and cilantro and stir so that everything is well coated in the sauce. Taste and add sea salt as needed.
2. Chill until you're ready to serve. Right before serving, add the avocado. This is best the day it's made, although it will keep in a sealed container in the refrigerator for 1 day.

Contramar'S Ceviche

Prep time: 5 minutes | Cook time: 15 minutes| Serves 6

- ½ red onion, thinly sliced lengthwise
- 1 tsp sea salt, plus 1 Tbsp
- 1½ lb / 650g sashimi-grade firm-fleshed white fish, such as halibut or mahi-mahi, filleted and cut into ½-inch / 12mm cubes
- 50g / ½ cup minced celery
- 2 serrano chiles, stemmed, seeded, veins removed (or not, depending on how spicy you want this to be), and sliced lengthwise into very thin strips
- 1 manzano chile, stemmed, seeded, veins removed (or not, depending on how spicy you want this to be), and sliced into thin rings
- 1 cup / 240ml freshly squeezed lime juice
- ½ cup / 10g cilantro leaves, coarsely chopped
- Drizzle of fresh cold-pressed olive oil
- Pinch of Maldon sea salt or another finishing salt
- Tortilla chips for serving

1. Place the onion in a bowl of cold water with the 1 tsp salt and let soak for 5 minutes, then drain.
2. In a bowl large enough to hold all of your ingredients, sprinkle the remaining 1 Tbsp salt over the fish and stir. Add the celery, serranos, and manzano and mix. Drain the onion and add to the bowl. Pour the lime juice over everything, sprinkle with the cilantro, and drizzle with the oil. Right before serving, add the finishing salt. Serve immediately with the tortilla chips to scoop up the fish.
3. Ceviche is at its prime the day it is made, so don't make more than you intend to serve and eat.

Mahi Mahi Ceviche with Ancho Chile and Hibiscus

Prep time: 5 minutes | Cook time: 15 minutes| Serves 6

- 1½ lb / 650g mahi-mahi, diced into bite-size pieces
- 1 tsp sea salt
- 2 Tbsp vegetable oil
- 1 ancho chile, stemmed, seeded, and cut into rings
- 1 oz / 30g whole organic dried hibiscus flowers
- 1 cup / 240ml freshly squeezed lime juice
- ¼ cup / 60ml olive oil
- 1 Tbsp diced chives
- 1 avocado, cut in half, pitted, peeled, and diced
- 1 tsp Maldon sea salt or another finishing salt

1. Place the mahi-mahi in a medium bowl and sprinkle with the sea salt. Line a plate with a brown paper bag.
2. In a small skillet over medium-high heat, warm the vegetable oil until it's hot but not sizzling. Add the ancho and fry for about 1 minute. Transfer the chile to the prepared plate to drain. Using the same pan and hot oil, fry the hibiscus flowers until crisp, then place them on the plate to drain. When the chile and hibiscus are cool enough to

handle, place them on a cutting board and chop them together until you have a deep red crumble of little bits and set aside.
3. To the bowl with the mahi-mahi, add the lime juice, olive oil, chives, and chile-hibiscus mixture and toss to combine. Add the avocado and finishing salt. Serve immediately.
4. Ceviche is at its prime the day it is made, so don't make more than you intend to serve and eat.

Salted Raw Shrimp Bathed In Lime, Chile, And Cilantro

Prep time: 5 minutes | Cook time: 15 minutes| Serves 6

- 1¼ lb / 575g raw medium-size shrimp, peeled, deveined, and butterflied
- 2 tsp sea salt, plus more as needed
- ½ red onion, thinly sliced lengthwise
- 1 cucumber, peeled, cut in half, and thinly sliced
- 1 cup / 240ml freshly squeezed lime juice
- ½ cup / 10g parsley leaves
- Packed ½ cup / 10g cilantro leaves
- ¼ cup / 60ml water
- 1 tsp chile tepín or chile piquín
- 2 Tbsp fresh cold-pressed olive oil
- Maldon sea salt or another finishing salt

1. Arrange the shrimp on a serving platter or individual plates (not a bowl). Sprinkle 1 tsp of the salt over the shrimp.
2. In a small bowl, sprinkle ½ tsp of the sea salt over the onion. (This will leach some of the moisture from the onion so that it's less crunchy.)
3. In another small bowl, sprinkle the remaining ½ tsp sea salt over the cucumber and add about 1 Tbsp of the lime juice.
4. In the jar of a blender, combine the parsley, cilantro, water, and remaining lime juice and liquefy. If it's frothy (which it probably will be), let it sit for about 5 minutes to settle.
5. Pour the contents of the blender over the shrimp and then scatter the onion and cucumber over the top. Drizzle with the oil and sprinkle with the finishing salt. Serve immediately.
6. Aguachile is at its prime the day it is made, so don't make more than you intend to serve and eat.

Chapter 8
Small Plates

Shrimp Ceviche from Nayarit

Prep time: 5 minutes | Cook time: 15 minutes| Serves 6

- 1 pound fresh shrimp, preferably the white Gulf variety, peeled, cleaned, and finely chopped
- 1 cup freshly squeezed lime juice (from 6 to 8 limes), plus more as needed
- ¼ red onion, finely chopped
- 1¾ teaspoons kosher salt, plus more as needed
- ½ cup grated carrots, grated on the large holes of a box grater
- ½ cup finely diced cucumber, peeled if desired
- 1 to 3 serrano chiles, finely chopped
- ¼ cup chopped fresh cilantro leaves
- 2 tablespoons sliced green onions
- Extra-virgin olive oil, for drizzling
- Tortilla chips or salted crackers, for serving

1. In a large bowl, combine the shrimp, lime juice, red onions, and salt. Let sit for 10 minutes, stirring occasionally.
2. Add the carrots, cucumber, chiles, cilantro, and green onions and stir to combine. Taste and adjust the lime juice and salt as needed. Drizzle lightly with olive oil and serve immediately with the chips.

Shrimp and Crab Ceviche with Tomatoes, Onions, and Jalapeños

Prep time: 5 minutes | Cook time: 5 minutes| Serves 6 to 8

- 1 cup plus 2 tablespoons freshly squeezed lime juice (from about 8 limes), or more as needed
- Salt
- 2 cups finely chopped cleaned shrimp (from about 1½ pounds), preferably the white Gulf variety
- ½ small white onion, finely diced
- 1 cup chilled Dungeness crab meat (from about 1 large crab)
- 2 jalapeños, finely chopped
- ½ bunch fresh cilantro leaves, chopped
- 2 cups small cherry tomatoes, halved, or chopped heirloom tomatoes
- Tortilla chips or salted crackers, for serving

1. Set a small pot of water on the stove and stir in 2 tablespoons lime juice; season generously with salt, so it tastes like the ocean, and bring to a boil. Add the shrimp and cook until just pink and opaque, 30 seconds to 1 minute. Strain and spread the shrimp pieces out in a single layer to dry and cool completely; chill. (At this point you can refrigerate the shrimp until ready to use, up to 2 days.)
2. In a medium serving bowl, combine the onion and the remaining 1 cup lime juice; let rest for 5 minutes, then add the shrimp and crab meat, jalapeños, and cilantro. Stir in the tomatoes just before serving. Taste and adjust the salt and lime juice as needed. Serve with the chips.

Halibut Ceviche with Red Chiles

Prep time: 5 minutes | Cook time: 35 minutes| Serves 4 to 6

- 2 medium dried árbol chiles, stemmed and seeded
- 3 dried guajillo chiles, stemmed and seeded
- 2 cups diced skinless halibut fillet
- Salt
- ½ cup freshly squeezed lime juice (from 3 to 4 limes), plus more as needed
- ¼ cup thinly sliced red onion
- 1 small jalapeño, finely chopped
- 2 tablespoons chopped fresh cilantro
- ⅓ cup diced firm-ripe avocado
- Tortilla chips, tortillas, or salted crackers, for serving

1. Place the árbol and guajillo chiles in a medium heatproof bowl and add enough boiling water to cover; let sit until the chiles are softened, about 20 minutes. Remove the chiles (reserve the soaking water) and transfer them to a blender or molcajete; puree to form a smooth paste, adding some of the soaking water as needed to blend.
2. Transfer the chile mixture to a medium bowl. When ready to serve, season the halibut with salt and stir it into the chile mixture along with the lime juice and red onions. Let rest for 5 minutes, then stir in the jalapeño and cilantro.
3. Transfer the ceviche to a serving bowl and top with the avocado. Serve immediately with the chips.

Baked Tortilla Chips Tossed with Spicy Salsa de Árbol

Prep time: 5 minutes | Cook time: 5 minutes| Serves 8

- 2 cups Salsa de Árbol
- 16 ounces homemade salted corn tortilla chips or thick, hearty store-bought chips
- 1 cup grated Cotija cheese
- ½ cup finely diced white onion
- ½ cup fresh cilantro leaves, finely chopped
- 1 cup sour cream
- Lime wedges, for serving

1. Be sure your salsa de árbol is prepared in advance and is still hot, or reheat on the stove. Preheat the oven to 450°F. Spread the chips on a baking sheet and bake until warmed through, about 2 minutes.
2. Transfer the chips from the oven to a large mixing bowl. Add the salsa and toss the chips with the hot salsa until they are completely covered. Transfer to a serving plate, then garnish the chips with the cheese, onion, and cilantro. Serve with the crema and lime wedges.

Green Ceviche with White Fish and Calamari

Prep time: 5 minutes | Cook time: 15 minutes | Serves 6 to 8

- 1½ pounds fresh, cleaned calamari, tentacles trimmed into bite-sized pieces, tubes cut into 1-inch squares
- Salt
- 12 medium tomatillos (about 2 pounds), husked, rinsed, dried, and halved
- Leaves from 1 large bunch cilantro (about 2½ cups)
- 2 to 3 jalapeños, finely chopped
- 3 cloves garlic, coarsely chopped
- 2 cups diced, skinned ling cod (rock cod) or other meaty white fish
- 1 cup freshly squeezed lime juice (from about 8 limes)
- Tortilla chips or salted crackers, for serving

1. Bring a medium pot of water to a boil. Meanwhile, set a medium bowl of ice water next to the stove. Season both the ice water and the pot of water generously with salt (both should taste as salty as the ocean). Once the water is boiling, add the calamari and let cook until firmed up slightly, 1½ to 2 minutes. Using a slotted spoon, quickly transfer the calamari to the ice water to cool. Remove when cold and drain well.
2. In a blender, combine the tomatillos, cilantro, jalapeños, garlic, and a pinch or two of salt; pulse until just chunky. Drain the mixture over a medium bowl and discard about two-thirds of the liquid (you should have a little less than 1 cup remaining). In a medium serving bowl, combine the remaining liquid with the chunky tomatillo mixture. (The recipe can be prepared to this point up to a day in advance; refrigerate the components separately.)
3. When ready to serve, in a separate medium bowl, combine the calamari, cod, and lime juice and let sit, stirring occasionally, for 5 minutes. Stir the fish mixture into the tomatillo mixture, then taste and adjust the amount of salt and lime juice. Serve immediately with the chips.

Hot Oaxacan and Jack Cheese Dip with Chorizo and Cactus

Prep time: 5 minutes | Cook time: 35 minutes | Serves 4

- 2 small nopales, spines trimmed away
- Salt
- 2 teaspoons rice bran oil or canola oil
- 6 ounces (¾ cup) crumbled store-bought Mexican chorizo (discard the casings)
- 1 cup shredded Jack cheese
- ⅔ cup shredded Oaxacan cheese
- Chopped cilantro leaves
- Tortilla chips or warm soft corn tortillas, for serving

1. Rinse the cactus leaves with cold water and pat them dry; season on both sides with salt. Preheat a skillet big enough to contain both cactus leaves over high heat (if they won't both fit, work in batches or in two separate skillets). Add the cactus leaves and cook, flipping them every 3 to 4 minutes, until well seared on both sides, about 15 minutes total. Transfer to a cutting board and let rest until cool enough to handle, then slice into thin, bite-sized strips.
2. Preheat the oven to 375°F. In a medium skillet, heat the oil over medium-high heat. Add the chorizo and cook, breaking up the meat into small pieces with a wooden spoon or spatula, until browned and cooked through, 6 to 8 minutes. Drain off any excess fat that pools in the bottom of the pan.
3. In a 16-ounce (6-inch) cazuela or other ovenproof baking dish, layer half of the Jack cheese evenly on the bottom. Top with a layer of the chorizo, then one-quarter of the Oaxacan cheese, the cactus strips, and the rest of the Jack and Oaxacan cheeses mixed together.
4. Set the dish on a baking sheet and bake until the cheese is completely melted and bubbling around the edges, about 10 minutes. Remove and garnish with cilantro leaves. Serve immediately with chips or tortillas for dipping.

Fruit Salad with Chile and Lime

Prep time: 5 minutes | Cook time: 5 minutes | Serves 4

- ¼ cup freshly squeezed lime juice (from 2 to 3 limes)
- ½ cup freshly squeezed orange juice (from 1 to 2 oranges)
- 1 teaspoon kosher salt
- 2 cups bite-sized watermelon cubes
- 4 cups bite-sized diced mixed melons or other tropical fruits of your choice, such as cantaloupe or pineapple
- ½ cup crumbled queso fresco
- 1 teaspoon Nopalito Spices
- 1 tablespoon Salsa "Bufalo"

1. In a large bowl, combine the lime juice, orange juice, and salt; whisk to dissolve the salt. Add the fruit and toss to coat in the citrus juice.
2. Transfer the fruit and all of the juices to a serving plate or bowl. Garnish with the queso fresco, Nopalito spices, and salsa.

Cactus Leaf Salad

Prep time: 5 minutes | Cook time: 35 minutes| Serves 4

- 3 medium nopales, spines trimmed away
- ¼ cup kosher salt, plus more as needed
- 12 slices red onion (from about ½ large onion)
- ¼ cup freshly squeezed lime juice (from 2 to 3 limes), divided
- 2 medium ripe tomatoes
- 1 avocado
- ¼ cup grated Cotija or ricotta salata cheese
- 1 tablespoon chopped fresh cilantro

1. Rinse the nopales and pat dry. Slice crosswise into ¼-inch strips and transfer to a colander set in the sink. Toss with ¼ cup kosher salt, then let macerate for about 30 minutes. Rinse the nopales under cold running water until most of the salt has been removed (this step will help minimize the sliminess of the cactus); drain well.
2. Meanwhile, in a large nonreactive skillet over medium heat, sauté the onions with 1 tablespoon of the lime juice and a pinch of salt, stirring occasionally, until the onions begin to turn pink, 2 to 3 minutes. Transfer to a small bowl, cover with plastic wrap, and let rest until cool.
3. When ready to serve, cut the tomatoes and avocado into ¼-inch cubes. In a serving bowl, gently toss the nopales, onions, tomatoes, avocados, and the remaining 3 tablespoons lime juice. Add salt to taste.
4. Divide the salad equally among four plates or arrange on a medium platter. Top with the cheese and cilantro.

Asparagus Quesadillas with Salsa Cilantro

Prep time: 5 minutes | Cook time: 25 minutes| Serves 4

- ¼ cup rice bran oil or canola oil, plus 1 teaspoon
- 2 cups thinly sliced white onions
- 4 cloves garlic
- 1 to 2 medium jalapeños, stemmed and finely chopped
- Salt
- 1 large bunch asparagus spears, woody ends trimmed away, remainder sliced into thin coins (4 cups)
- 4 homemade soft corn tortillas or 8 store-bought soft corn tortillas
- 1½ cups (12 ounces) shredded Oaxacan cheese or Jack cheese
- For serving
- Crumbled queso fresco
- Fresh cilantro leaves
- Salsa Cilantro

1. To make the filling, in a medium skillet, heat the oil over medium-high heat. Add the onions, garlic, and jalapeños and season with salt. Cook, stirring occasionally, until the onions are translucent, 3 to 4 minutes. Stir in the asparagus, then turn off the heat and let cool slightly.
2. Preheat a griddle or large skillet over medium heat and drizzle the pan with about 1 teaspoon of oil. Add all of the homemade or 4 of the store-bought tortillas, working in batches as needed to fit. If using homemade, distribute a scant ⅓ cup cheese over half of each, then divide the asparagus mixture evenly, placing it over the cheese; fold the tortillas in half to cover the filling. If using store-bought tortillas, spread a layer of cheese (about 3 tablespoons) over the top of one whole tortilla, top with the asparagus and about 2 tablespoons more of the cheese, then top with a second whole tortilla. Cook, flipping the quesadillas once or twice, until the cheese is fully melted, 6 to 8 minutes total. Repeat with the remaining quesadillas as needed.
3. Transfer the quesadillas to four plates and garnish with the queso fresco and fresh cilantro. Serve with the cilantro salsa.

Cucumber and Purslane Salad

Prep time: 5 minutes | Cook time: 15 minutes| Serves 4

- ½ cup pepitas
- ½ cup freshly squeezed lemon juice (from 2 to 3 lemons)
- ¼ cup apple cider vinegar
- 1 cup extra-virgin olive oil
- 1 cup rice bran oil or canola oil
- Salt
- 4 cups cucumber, halved lengthwise and sliced into thick half-moons
- ¼ cup freshly squeezed lime juice (from 2 to 3 limes)
- 4 cups cleaned purslane or watercress
- 1 avocado, pitted, peeled, and diced
- 1 cup crumbled queso fresco, for garnish

1. To make the dressing, preheat the oven to 350°F. Place the pepitas on a small baking sheet and roast until browned in places and aromatic, about 10 minutes. Remove and let cool completely.
2. Place half of the fully cooled pepitas in a food processor and grind into a coarse powder. Add the lemon juice and vinegar and mix thoroughly. With the motor running, slowly stream in both oils until the dressing is completely emulsified. Season with salt to taste.
3. Place the cucumber and lime juice in a large serving bowl and let marinate 5 minutes. Stir to distribute the lime juice, then add the purslane, avocado, and dressing to taste and toss gently to combine. Garnish with the queso fresco and the remaining ¼ cup of the toasted pepitas.

Little Gem Salad with Apples and Jalapeño Vinaigrette

Prep time: 5 minutes | Cook time: 15 minutes| Serves 4 to 6

- ¼ red onion, thinly sliced
- 1 small jalapeño, smoked if desired
- ¼ cup freshly squeezed lime juice (from 2 to 3 limes), divided
- ¼ teaspoon kosher salt, plus more for seasoning
- Rice bran oil or canola oil, for deep-frying
- 2 soft corn tortillas (if using homemade, use 1-day-old), sliced into ¼-inch strips
- ¼ cup apple cider vinegar
- ½ cup extra-virgin olive oil
- ½ cup rice bran oil or canola oil
- 8 cups Little Gem lettuces
- 1 firm-ripe apple (Granny Smith or another tart variety), thinly sliced
- 6 radishes, very thinly sliced
- 1 avocado, pitted, peeled, and diced
- ½ cup Spiced Peanuts or a spicy store-bought version
- Shaved ricotta salata cheese, for garnish

1. Bring a small pot of water to a boil. Place the red onions in a small heatproof bowl and ladle some boiling water over to cover; let sit 5 minutes. Meanwhile, if you did not smoke the jalapeño, add it to the boiling water; boil until the chile is slightly softened and darkened, 8 to 10 minutes. Remove and let cool.
2. Drain the red onions and add 2 tablespoons of the lime juice and the ¼ teaspoon salt to the bowl; let sit so the onions pickle slightly, about 40 minutes. The onions should look pink at this point.
3. Set a paper towel–lined plate next to the stove. Use a deep fryer, or add enough of the oil to a medium pot so it comes 1 to 2 inches up the sides of the pan. Heat the oil until it registers 350°F on a deep-fat thermometer, then add the tortilla strips, working in batches if necessary to make sure they are completely submerged. Fry, turning occasionally, until very crispy, 5 to 8 minutes. Remove using a slotted spoon or spider and transfer to the prepared plate; season with salt while still warm.
4. To make the vinaigrette, transfer the jalapeño to a blender and add the vinegar and the remaining 2 tablespoons lime juice; blend until smooth. With the motor running, stream in the oils until emulsified; season with salt to taste.
5. In a large serving bowl, combine the lettuces, apple, and avocado; season with salt to taste and toss with ¼ cup plus 2 tablespoons of the vinaigrette (or more to taste). Garnish with the spiced peanuts and ricotta salata, the pickled onions, and the fried tortilla strips.

Fried Chickpeas with Chili Powder

Prep time: 5 minutes | Cook time: 2 hours 15 minutes|Makes 4 cups

- 4 cups dried chickpeas
- 5 tablespoons kosher salt, divided
- 2 quarts rice bran oil or canola oil
- 2 tablespoons store-bought Mexican chili powder

1. Preheat the oven to 350°F. Add the chickpeas to a large ovenproof pot, then fill with water. Add 3 tablespoons of the salt, cover the pot, transfer to the oven, and bake for 2 hours. Remove and drain completely in a colander. Let the chickpeas cool.
2. Set a medium-large heatproof bowl next to the stove. Add the oil to a large, deep-sided skillet or pot, and heat until it registers 350°F on a deep-fat thermometer. Add the chickpeas and let cook until golden-brown and crunchy, about 15 minutes.
3. Using a slotted spoon or spider skimmer, remove the chickpeas and transfer them to the bowl. While they're still hot, mix them with the chili powder and the remaining 3 tablespoons salt. Let cool completely and serve. Will keep for 7 to 10 days stored in an airtight container.

Pico de Gallo

Prep time: 5 minutes | Cook time: 10 minutes|Makes about 1½ cups

- ½ small red onion, finely diced
- 2 tablespoons freshly squeezed lime juice (from 1 to 2 limes)
- Salt
- 3 red tomatoes, finely diced
- 2 tablespoons chopped cilantro leaves
- 2 jalapeños, diced
- ½ bunch scallions, thinly sliced

1. In a medium bowl, stir together the red onion, lime juice, and a pinch of salt; let sit 5 minutes.
2. Add the tomatoes, cilantro, jalapeños, and scallions. Taste and adjust the seasoning as needed.

Crispy Red Quesadillas with Braised Red Pork and Pork Rinds

Prep time: 5 minutes | Cook time: 2 hours 25 minutes| Serves 4

- Quesadillas
- 1 pound boneless pork shoulder
- Salt
- ½ cup Salsa Para Quesadillas (recipe follows), plus more for serving
- 4 homemade soft ancho-corn tortillas or 8 store-bought corn tortillas
- 1½ cups (12 ounces) shredded Oaxacan cheese or Jack cheese
- ¼ cup rice bran oil or canola oil
- For serving
- Chicharrónes (recipe follows; optional)
- Crumbled queso fresco
- Fresh cilantro leaves
- Finely chopped white onion

1. Place the pork shoulder in a medium pot and fill with water to cover; season the water generously with salt. Bring to a boil, then reduce to a steady simmer and let cook until the meat is tender, about 2 hours. Drain, then shred the meat and mix with the ½ cup salsa.
2. Preheat a griddle or large skillet over medium heat, and wipe it with a thin layer of oil. Working in batches as needed for fit, cook the tortillas, flipping every 3 minutes, until puffed, about 9 minutes total.
3. Sprinkle one-quarter of the cheese on top of each tortilla, then distribute a scant ½ cup of pork evenly over the top; fold the tortillas in half to cover the filling. (If using store-bought tortillas, which are a bit smaller, spread the cheese and pork over the top of one whole tortilla, then top each with a second tortilla.) Pour about 2 tablespoons oil on top of each homemade tortilla, or 1 tablespoon on each store-bought, letting some of the oil run around the edges and onto the pan. Cook, flipping the quesadillas as needed to crisp both sides in the oil and melt the cheese, 6 to 10 minutes total.
4. Transfer the quesadillas to four plates and add about ¼ cup chicharrónes, if using, to each quesadilla. Garnish with the queso fresco, cilantro, and onions to taste.

Fish Tacos Marinated in Adobo

Prep time: 5 minutes | Cook time: 15 minutes|Makes 8

- 1 pound skinless snapper cod, or halibut fillets
- Salt
- 2 tablespoons Adobo Paste (recipe follows)
- Rice bran oil or canola oil,for sautéing
- For serving
- 8 warm homemade soft corn tortillas or store-bought soft corn tortillas
- Diced white onion

- Chopped fresh cilantro
- Small orange wedges or finely chopped pineapple
- Salsa de Morita con Tomatillo

1. Cut the fish into thin 2-ounce pieces (about 5 inches long); season with salt and coat with the adobo. Cover and let marinate at least 2 hours and up to overnight.
2. In a large skillet or on a griddle, heat 2 to 3 tablespoons oil over medium-high heat. Once the oil is hot, add the fish and cook until seared on one side, about 3 minutes. Turn and cook on the remaining side until just cooked through, about 3 minutes more.
3. Divide the fish among the warm tortillas. Garnish with the onions, cilantro, oranges, and salsa.

Toasted Corn with Crema, Ground Chile, and Queso Fresco

Prep time: 5 minutes | Cook time: 10 minutes| Serves 4

- Kernels cut from 3 ears fresh corn (about 4 cups)
- 2 tablespoons freshly squeezed lime juice (from 1 to 2 limes), plus 4 lime wedges, for serving
- 1 teaspoon kosher salt, plus more to taste
- ½ cup Crema or sour cream
- ½ cup crumbled queso fresco
- 1½ teaspoons each ground chili powder and smoked paprika
- ¼ cup Pico de Gallo (recipe follows)

1. In a large skillet or griddle over high heat, cook the corn kernels, stirring occasionally, until lightly charred in places, about 5 minutes (be careful, as the corn may start "jumping"; lower the heat as needed). Stir in the lime juice and salt. Taste and adjust the seasoning and acidity as needed.
2. Divide the corn kernels among four individual bowls or place in one large serving bowl and top with the crema, queso fresco, Nopalito spices, and pico de gallo. Serve with lime wedges, and stir the toppings into the corn just before eating.

Quesadillas with Brussels Sprouts and Cascabel Chile Oil

Prep time: 5 minutes | Cook time: 35 minutes| Serves 4

- Cascabel Chile Oil
- 6 dried cascabel chiles, stemmed and seeded
- 1 dried guajillo chile, stemmed and seeded
- 1½ cups rice bran oil or canola oil
- 1 small clove garlic
- Quesadillas
- ¼ cup rice bran oil or canola oil, plus more as needed
- 2 cups thinly sliced white onions
- 4 cups cored, thinly sliced Brussels sprouts (about 1 pound)
- Kosher salt
- 4 homemade soft corn tortillas or 8 store-bought soft corn tortillas
- 1½ cups (12 ounces) shredded Oaxacan cheese or Jack cheese
- For serving
- Crumbled queso fresco
- Fresh cilantro leaves
- Salsa Macha (optional)

1. To make the chile oil, preheat the oven to 350°F. Place the cascabel and guajillo chiles on a baking sheet and roast until the guajillos turn dark red, about 5 minutes; remove, but do not turn off the oven.
2. Meanwhile, bring a small pot of water to a boil. Transfer the chiles to a medium heatproof bowl and cover with boiling water; let sit until the chiles are soft, about 20 minutes.
3. Drain the chiles and place them in a blender along with the 1½ cups oil and the garlic; blend until the oil becomes clear and red. Once it is fully cooled, the cascabel oil can be stored in an airtight container until ready to use.
4. To make the filling, in a large skillet, heat the ¼ cup oil over high heat. Add the onions and lower the heat to medium-high; cook, stirring occasionally, until softened and lightly browned in places, 5 to 6 minutes. Add the Brussels sprouts and season with salt; let cook, stirring occasionally, until the size of the leaves is reduced by half and their edges are beginning to brown, 5 to 7 minutes. Drizzle with 2 to 4 tablespoons of the chile oil to taste, and season with more salt as needed.
5. Preheat a large skillet or griddle to medium-high heat. Add all of the homemade or half of the store-bought tortillas, working in batches as needed to fit. Sprinkle the shredded cheese over one side of the homemade tortillas or across the full diameter of the store-bought ones. Quickly divide the Brussels sprouts mixture over the top (about ⅓ cup per quesadilla). Fold the homemade tortillas in half to cover; top store-bought tortillas with another whole tortilla to cover. Cook, flipping the quesadilla 1 to 2 times with a spatula, until the cheese is fully melted, 5 to 7 minutes total. Repeat with the remaining quesadillas as needed.
6. Transfer the quesadillas to four plates and garnish with the queso fresco and cilantro. Serve with the salsa macha if using.

Marinated Shredded Pork Tacos

Prep time: 5 minutes | Cook time: 15 minutes| Serves 6 to 8

- Pork
- 5 pounds boneless pork shoulder
- Kosher salt
- Recado Rojo (recipe follows)
- 1 banana leaf (optional)
- 1 cup (8 ounces) canned diced tomatoes and their juices
- ½ cup freshly squeezed orange juice (from 1 to 2 oranges)
- ½ cup freshly squeezed lime juice (from about 4 limes)
- ½ white onion
- 5 cloves garlic
- 2 bay leaves
- ¼ bunch fresh epazote, basil, or cilantro
- For serving
- 16 to 20 warm homemade soft corn tortillas or store-bought soft corn tortillas
- Fresh cilantro
- Thinly sliced red onions
- Habanero Salsa

1. Season the pork generously with salt, then marinate it with the recado rojo for at least 4 hours or up to overnight.
2. If using the banana leaf, heat a griddle or large skillet to medium heat and briefly cook the leaf, turning once and rotating as needed, until lightly toasted and softened, about 5 seconds per side. Transfer to a small roasting pan allowing it to hang off the side.
3. Preheat the oven to 300°F. In a medium bowl, combine the tomatoes, orange juice, and lime juice. Place the pork in the roasting pan (laying it atop half of the banana leaf, if using), then pour the tomato mixture over the top. Distribute the onion, garlic, bay leaves, and epazote in the pan, and fold the banana leaf over the pork to cover; cover the pan with foil. Place in the oven and let braise until the meat is very tender, about 3 hours. Remove from the oven and let cool slightly, then shred the meat into small pieces. Taste and adjust the seasoning as needed.
4. Top each tortilla with as much meat as you like. Garnish with cilantro and onions, and Habanero salsa to taste, keeping in mind that the salsa is quite spicy.

Recado Rojo

Prep time: 5 minutes | Cook time: 55 minutes|Makes 2 cups

- ¼ cup plus 1 tablespoon annatto seeds (achiote)
- 1½ teaspoons dried oregano
- 1½ teaspoons freshly ground black pepper
- 1½ teaspoons ground cumin
- ½ teaspoon ground cinnamon
- 5 cloves garlic, peeled
- 1 dried ancho chile, stemmed and seeded
- ½ teaspoon white vinegar
- ⅓ cup plus 1 tablespoon freshly squeezed orange juice (from about 1 orange)
- ¼ cup freshly squeezed lime juice (from about 2 limes)
- 2 teaspoons rice bran oil or canola oil
- Kosher salt

1. Place the annatto seeds in a small pot and cover with water. Bring to a boil, then turn off the heat and let sit for 1 hour.
2. Meanwhile, preheat the oven to 350°F. Distribute the oregano, pepper, cumin, cinnamon, and garlic on a small baking sheet. Bake, stirring the spices around on the baking sheet halfway through, until the mixture is toasted and aromatic, about 20 minutes.
3. In a medium heatproof bowl, cover the ancho chile with boiling water; let sit until softened, about 20 minutes, then strain.
4. Using a slotted spoon, transfer the annatto seeds to a blender (reserve the soaking water). Add the toasted spices, chile, vinegar, orange and lime juices, and a generous pinch of salt. Blend, streaming in the oil to form a thick, smooth paste and adding some of the soaking water from the achiote as needed.

Sweet Potato Tamales with Mole Amarillo

Prep time: 5 minutes | Cook time: 1 hour 15 minutes|Makes about 24

- 2 medium whole sweet potatoes, peeled, plus 6 cups ½-inch-diced sweet potatoes
- Olive oil
- 7 cups masa prepared from store-bought masa harina
- 3 cups (6 sticks) unsalted butter, softened
- 1 tablespoon kosher salt, plus more as needed
- 1 teaspoon baking powder
- ½ white onion, chopped
- 1 jalapeño, thinly sliced
- 1 clove garlic, peeled and chopped
- 2 cups Mole Amarillo (recipe follows)
- 20 large corn husks or 40 small ones

1. To make the filling, preheat the oven to 350°F. Rub the whole sweet potatoes with olive oil and wrap them together in foil; place on a large baking sheet and bake until extremely soft, about 1 hour 15 minutes. About halfway through baking, place the diced sweet potatoes on the baking sheet and roast until al dente, 20 to 30 minutes.
2. Quarter the whole sweet potatoes and puree in a food processor.
3. Place 1 cup of the puree in the bowl of a stand mixer fitted with the paddle attachment. Add half each of the masa, butter, salt, and baking powder and beat until well combined. (Alternatively, you can mix the ingredients by hand, but the stand mixer creates an airier result.) Transfer this mixture to a larger bowl, then repeat the mixer processing with another 1 cup of the potato puree and the remaining masa, butter, salt, and baking powder. Combine with the first batch, then taste and adjust the seasoning as needed (it should taste well-seasoned). Discard any remaining potato puree or save for another use.
4. To make the chunky sweet potato filling, in a medium skillet, heat 1 tablespoon olive oil over high heat. Add the onion, jalapeño, and garlic and season with salt; cook, stirring occasionally, until the onions are translucent, 4 to 5 minutes. (Turn down the heat as needed so the onions don't start to brown.)
5. In a large mixing bowl, combine the onion mixture, the roasted diced potatoes, and 2 cups of the mole amarillo. Taste and add more salt as needed.
6. To make the tamales, soak the corn husks in very hot water until softened, about 20 minutes. Remove from the water (no need to dry them off). Working with one at a time, lay a husk on a clean work surface with the curved side facing up and the narrower end facing you. (Some husks will be smaller than others—if necessary, use two small husks together, overlapping their long edges slightly.) Using a spoon or your hands and leaving a 1½-inch border clear along the wide, flat end of the husks, place a heaping ¼ cup of masa over the center of each corn husk. Spread the masa out to form a round about 3 inches across. Add about ¼ cup of the chunky sweet potato filling in a line down the center of the masa, then fold the long edges of the corn husk over the filling to cover. Finally, fold the pointy end of the husk over to form a packet (the opposite end of the tamal should remain open). Tamales can be filled up to 2 days in advance of steaming. You can also freeze them at this point; add an extra 15 minutes of steaming time if starting with frozen ones.
7. Transfer the tamales to a steamer, piling them as needed to fit, either horizontally or with their open ends facing up. Steam until the masa has firmed, 60 to 90 minutes. (To test, open the husk: a toothpick inserted into the masa should come out mostly clean.)

Tamales with Stewed Chicken

Prep time: 5 minutes | Cook time: 1 hour 55 minutes | Makes about 24

- Chicken Filling
- 1 whole (3- to 3½-pound) chicken
- ½ white onion
- 3 cloves garlic
- 5 bay leaves
- 7 dried guajillo chiles, stemmed and seeded
- 12 dried chiles de árbol, stemmed and seeded
- ½ cinnamon stick
- ½ teaspoon cumin seeds
- ½ teaspoon dried thyme
- ½ teaspoon ground ginger
- ½ teaspoon dried marjoram
- 5 whole cloves
- 5 allspice berries
- 1 tablespoon sesame seeds
- 3 cups (24 ounces) canned diced tomatoes and their juices
- ¼ cup white vinegar
- ¼ cup rice bran oil or canola oil
- 1½ ounces (half a 3.1-ounce disk) Mexican chocolate (preferably Ibarra or Abuelita brand), chopped
- Salt
- Tamales
- 6 cups masa prepared from store-bought masa harina
- 2 cups lard or softened unsalted butter (4 sticks)
- 1 teaspoon baking powder
- 1 tablespoon kosher salt, plus more as needed
- 24 large corn husks or 48 small ones

1. To prepare the chicken, place it in a large pot and add enough water to just cover it. Add the onion, garlic, and bay leaves and bring to a boil, then reduce to a simmer and let cook, skimming the foam and fat off the top occasionally, until the meat is just cooked through, about 45 minutes. Remove the chicken (reserve the cooking liquid for another use if desired) and let cool slightly; finely shred the meat into small pieces. Set aside or refrigerate until ready to use.

2. Preheat the oven to 350°F. Place all of the dried chiles in a medium heatproof bowl and cover with boiling water; let sit until the chiles are softened, about 20 minutes. Meanwhile, combine the cinnamon, cumin, thyme, ginger, marjoram, cloves, allspice, and sesame seeds on a baking sheet and bake until toasted, about 10 minutes.

3. Transfer the spices and the softened chiles (discard the soaking water) to a blender. Add the tomatoes and vinegar and blend until smooth. Pour the mixture into a large pot and bring to a boil; reduce to a simmer and let cook for 30 minutes.

4. When you're ready to assemble the tamales, fry the salsa: In a large pot, heat the oil over high heat. Pour in the salsa quickly and all at once (be careful, as the oil may splatter) and bring to a boil; add the chocolate and season with salt. The mixture should be thin; if necessary, add some of the reserved chicken cooking liquid or water. The salsa can be prepared to this point up to 3 days in advance if then cooled completely and refrigerated.

5. Combine the chicken with just enough salsa to cover and saturate it. Reserve the remaining salsa for serving alongside the tamales.

6. To make the tamales, in the bowl of a stand mixer fitted with the paddle attachment, combine the masa, lard, baking powder, and salt; beat until well blended. (Alternatively, you can stir the ingredients by hand in a large bowl, but the mixer will make the masa lighter and airier.)

7. To assemble, soak the corn husks in very hot water until softened, about 20 minutes. Remove from the water (no need to dry them off). Working with one at a time, lay a husk on a clean work surface with the curved side facing up and the narrower end facing you. (Some husks will be smaller than others—if necessary, use two small husks together, overlapping their long edges slightly.) Using a spoon or your hands and leaving a 1½-inch border clear along the wide, flat end of the husk, place a heaping ¼ cup of masa in the center of the corn husk, then spread it to form a circle about 3 inches across. Add about ¼ cup of the chicken filling to the center of the masa, then fold the long edges of the corn husk over the filling to cover. Fold the pointy end of the husk over to form a packet (the opposite end of the tamal should remain open). Tamales can be filled up to 2 days in advance of steaming. You can also freeze them at this point; add an extra 15 minutes of steaming time if starting with frozen ones.

8. Transfer the tamales to a steamer, piling them as needed to fit, either horizontally or with their open ends facing up. Steam until the masa has firmed, 60 to 90 minutes. (To test, open the husk: a toothpick inserted into the masa should come out mostly clean.)

9. To serve, open the tamales and spoon some of the extra salsa on top if desired.

Chapter 9
Main Dishes

Mussels In Chipotle Sauce

Prep time: 5 minutes | Cook time: 5 minutes| Serves 6

- ¼ cup / 60ml olive oil
- 1 cup / 140g finely minced shallots
- 1 tsp sea salt, plus more as needed
- 2 garlic cloves, pressed or mashed with a mortar and pestle
- 1 cup / 240ml white wine
- 1½ cups / 360ml shrimp stock or Fish Stock
- 4 lb / 1.8kg mussels, well scrubbed so that no grit or beards remain
- ¼ cup / 60g Mexican Sour Cream
- 2 Tbsp adobo from canned chipotles in adobo or 2 whole chipotles
- Chopped parsley
- Crusty bread

1. Heat the oil in a large heavy-bottom stockpot over medium-high heat until it's shimmering but not smoking. Add the shallots and cook until they're translucent but not browned. Add the salt, then add the garlic and sauté for just 1 minute, until you can smell it. Add the wine, bring to a boil, and let boil for about 2 minutes before adding the stock. Return to a boil, add the mussels, and cover the pot. As soon as the majority of the mussels open, which should take only a few minutes, turn off the heat. Any mussels that don't open should be discarded.
2. Combine the crema and adobo or chipotles in a small bowl. Stir the chipotle mixture into the broth.
3. Serve the mussels immediately in individual bowls, dividing the sauce evenly over the mussels. Garnish each portion with a scattering of parsley. Enjoy with a hunk of bread.

Grilled Octopus with Black Salsa

Prep time: 5 minutes | Cook time: 15 minutes| Serves 4

- 1 cooked octopus
- 2 to 4 Tbsp Black Salsa (2 Tbsp per 1 lb / 455g of octopus)

1. Coat the octopus in the salsa negra, rubbing it all over. Oil your grill and heat it to high or oil a grill pan and place it over high heat. Place the octopus on the heated grill or grill pan and let it cook on each side for a few minutes. You are not cooking the meat, just heating it through and giving it a chance to absorb and cook the sauce a little more.
2. When the octopus has nice grill marks and the heat of the grill has fused the sauce with the octopus, transfer it to a cutting board and let it rest for 5 to 10 minutes. Chop into pieces and serve warm. It's best eaten on the day it's cooked.

Black Rice

Prep time: 5 minutes | Cook time: 25 minutes| Serves 6

- ½ cup / 120ml olive oil
- 1 white onion, minced
- 1 garlic clove, pressed or mashed with a mortar and pestle
- 1 green bell pepper, diced
- 1 red bell pepper, diced
- 1½ cups / 150g cleaned and quartered cremini or white mushrooms
- ¾ lb / 340g squid, cleaned and cut into rings
- 1 oz / 30ml sherry, tequila, or mezcal
- 2 tsp sea salt
- 2 cups / 480ml Fish Stock
- 2 Tbsp squid ink
- 2 cups / 400g bomba or Arborio rice
- ¼ tsp ground nutmeg
- 2 jalapeños, stemmed and minced
- 1 recipe Chipotle Mayonnaise

1. Warm the oil over medium heat in a Dutch oven or paella pan. Once it's shimmering but not smoking, add the onion and fry for 3 to 4 minutes, until it looks translucent but not browned. Then add the garlic, bell peppers, and mushrooms, and fry for an additional 1 to 2 minutes. Once you can smell the garlic and the mushrooms have softened, throw in the squid, and add the sherry, tequila, or mezcal and the salt. Cook everything for 4 to 5 minutes. While this mixture cooks, bring your stock to a boil in a small saucepan.
2. Add the boiling stock to the pot with the vegetables and the squid. Decrease the heat to low, add the squid ink, and simmer to dissolve it into the stock. Add the rice and the nutmeg and continue to simmer for 20 minutes, until almost all of the liquid has been absorbed into the cooking rice. You shouldn't stir it, but you can use a spoon or spatula to nudge the broth under the rice occasionally.
3. In the last 5 minutes of the simmering time, preheat the broiler.
4. Once the rice has just absorbed the broth but is still quite moist, remove the pan from the stove top and place it under the broiler for 2 minutes, just to crisp the top.
5. Sprinkle with the parsley and jalapeño and serve immediately, passing the mayonnaise at the table.

Fish and Tortillas In Red Salsa

Prep time: 5 minutes | Cook time: 15 minutes| Serves 6

- Tomato Sauce
- 2 Tbsp olive oil
- 1 white onion, coarsely chopped
- 1 habanero chile, stemmed, seeded, veins removed (or not, depending on how spicy you want this to be), and chopped
- 1 garlic clove, chopped
- 4 Roma tomatoes, cored, blanched in boiling water for 30 seconds, peeled, and chopped or 4 canned whole tomatoes
- 1 Tbsp tomato paste (optional; use only if the tomatoes are at all pink)
- ½ tsp sea salt, plus more if needed
- Pinch of freshly ground white pepper
- 2 cups / 480g Refried Beans
- 1¼ lb / 575g "Fish-A-Dillas"
- ¼ cup / 60ml safflower oil
- 8 to 12 Corn Tortillas
- 6 padron or habanero peppers
- 1 recipe Pickled Red Onions

1. To make the sauce: Warm the olive oil in a skillet over medium heat until it's hot but not smoking. Add the onion and chile and cook until the onion is translucent. Add the garlic and cook for 1 minute more, just until you can smell its fragrance. Add the tomatoes, tomato paste, salt, and pepper and simmer over low heat for about 5 minutes, until it reduces a bit. Taste and add more salt, if needed.
2. In separate pans, warm the refried beans and pescadillas fillings over low heat.
3. Once your filling, tomato sauce, and beans are all hot and you're ready to serve this dish, heat the safflower oil in a skillet over medium-high heat until it's shimmering. Line a plate with a brown paper bag. Fry the tortillas one at a time in the oil, flipping them so that each side gets golden and they puff slightly. Place them on the plate to drain.
4. On the ungreased comal or in a skillet over high heat, cook the padron or habanero peppers until blistered on all sides, about 3 minutes.
5. To serve, place a tortilla on a plate and spread it with 1 to 2 Tbsp of the beans. Top with 1 to 2 Tbsp of the filling. Place another fried tortilla on top of it and ladle the sauce over. Garnish with a sprinkling of pickled onions and a padron pepper and serve immediately.

Shredded Chicken In Tomato Chipotle Sauce

Prep time: 5 minutes | Cook time: 25 minutes| Serves 6

- 6 Roma tomatoes, cored and cut in half
- 4 garlic cloves
- 1 cup / 240ml Chicken Stock (or use the chicken-poaching water plus a few aromatics and vegetables)
- 2 canned chipotles in adobo, plus more if desired
- 2 tsp sea salt, plus more as needed
- ¼ cup / 60ml safflower oil

- 3 large white onions, slivered
- 2 poached boneless, skinless chicken breasts, finely shredded

1. In the jar of a blender, combine the tomatoes, garlic, stock, chipotles, and 1 tsp of the salt and liquefy.
2. Over high heat, warm the oil in a large heavy-bottom skillet or medium saucepan. Add the onions, making sure they sizzle when they hit the pan. You want them to cook at a high enough heat that they are frying and not caramelizing, so they retain a slight crunch rather than becoming soft and sweet. Add the remaining 1 tsp salt and cook until the onions are golden brown.
3. Pour the contents of the blender into the pan of onions and bring to a boil. Decrease the heat and simmer for 5 to 10 minutes, until the sauce has thickened. Add the chicken and cook briefly, just until the chicken has absorbed some of the sauce and heated through. Taste and add more salt if needed.
4. Tinga de pollo tastes great as a taco topping, an enchilada filling, or served on its own with rice and beans. It can be stored in a sealed container in the refrigerator for up to 5 days, and in fact, it tastes even better reheated than when it's first made.

Ground Beef Hash

Prep time: 5 minutes | Cook time: 45 minutes| Serves 6

- 2 Tbsp lard
- ½ lb / 230g ground beef
- 2 tsp sea salt
- ½ white onion, minced
- 1 carrot, minced
- 2 garlic cloves, minced
- Pinch of ground cumin
- 1 cup / 240ml beef stock

1. In a medium skillet over medium-high heat, heat the lard until it's bubbling. Drop quarter-size pieces of ground beef into the pan and let them sear, turning the chunks over with a spatula so they brown on all sides. Add 1 tsp of the salt. Once the chunks of beef are browned (but not thoroughly cooked), use a slotted spoon to transfer them from the pan to a plate. Don't rinse out the pan.
2. In the same pan used to sear the beef, fry the onion and carrot. Once the onion is golden and the carrot has softened, add the remaining 1 tsp salt, the garlic, and cumin and cook while stirring for about 1 minute, until you can smell the spices toasting. Return the meat to the pan. Add the stock and use a large wooden spoon or potato masher to break the meat into smaller pieces. Cover the pan and let it simmer for about 10 minutes so that the flavors meld together. Remove the lid and cook for another 2 minutes, until most of the liquid has been absorbed and/or has evaporated.
3. As a final step, stir in the salsa for added flavor, if desired.
4. Store in the refrigerator for up 3 days. To reheat, warm in a skillet over low heat.

Chicken In Tomatillo Salsa with Cilantro

Prep time: 5 minutes | Cook time: 45 minutes| Serves 6

- ¼ cup / 60ml safflower oil, plus more if needed
- 1 garlic clove
- 1 whole chicken, cut into 6 pieces
- 3 Yukon gold potatoes, peeled or not, cut into large (1- to 2-inch / 2.5 to 5cm) chunks
- ½ white onion, finely diced
- 2 cups / 480ml Green Salsa
- 1 cup / 20g cilantro leaves, finely chopped
- 1 recipe Rice

1. Warm the oil in a 4 qt / 3.8L Dutch oven or heavy-bottom stockpot over medium-high heat. Skewer the garlic clove on the tines of a fork and swivel it through the hot oil. The oil should be hot enough that the garlic sizzles and turns golden. Once this happens, remove the garlic and set it aside (don't throw it away).
2. Add 2 or 3 chicken pieces, skin-side down, to the hot oil. Don't overcrowd the pan. You are not cooking the chicken through, just searing it, allowing the skin to brown slightly, which brings out the flavor when it stews. The chicken skin will stick at first, but will release fairly easily once it's done searing. Using tongs or a slotted spoon, flip each piece of chicken to sear the other side. Then remove the seared chicken and set aside on a plate while you continue to sear the rest of the pieces on each side. Set it all aside while you cook the potatoes.
3. Using the hot oil in the bottom of the pan (add a bit more, if needed), brown the potato chunks just as you did the chicken, adding them in a single layer and allowing them to turn golden on each side before flipping them. You are not cooking the potatoes through, just searing them; this also helps bring out their flavor and keeps them from falling apart in the stew. Once they're a light golden color, remove them and set them on a plate.
4. Now take that clove of garlic that you used to swivel in the oil before you cooked your chicken and slice it fairly thinly. Add the sliced garlic to the oil in the pan, along with the onion, and sauté until soft and lightly browned. Strictly speaking, you could skip this step, since the salsa has plenty of flavor, but I really like the texture of the minced onion.
5. Add the salsa to the pot, along with the chicken pieces and potatoes. Bring it to a boil, cover, decrease the heat, and simmer for about 30 minutes. Cut into a thick piece of chicken and chunk of potato to confirm they're cooked through.
6. Sprinkle the cilantro over the stew. To serve, scoop the rice into bowls and spoon the stew over the rice. The tinga can be stored in a sealed container in the refrigerator for 3 to 5 days.

Beef Tongue In Morita Chile Salsa

Prep time: 5 minutes | Cook time: about 4 hours| Serves 6

- 1 (3 to 4 lb / 1.4 to 1.8kg) beef tongue
- 1 bay leaf (preferably fresh)
- 1 Tbsp coriander seeds
- 1 Tbsp black peppercorns
- 2 chiles de árbol, stemmed, seeded, and torn in half
- 2 or 3 sprigs thyme or 1 Tbsp dried
- 2 or 3 sprigs oregano or 1 Tbsp dried
- 2 Tbsp sea salt
- 4 garlic cloves
- 1 Tbsp safflower oil
- ½ white onion, minced
- 1 recipe Morita Chile Salsa

1. To cook the tongue: Preheat the oven to 325°F / 165°C. Place the tongue in a small to medium heavy-bottom stockpot, in which it just fits snugly. Add the bay leaf, coriander, peppercorns, chiles, thyme, oregano, salt, and garlic, then cover with water. Bring to a boil and then place aluminum foil or an oven-safe lid on the pot and put it in the oven for 3 to 4 hours. After 2 hours, check the temperature of the cooked tongue with a meat thermometer; when the meat is done the temperature should be 160°F / 70°C. You can also test for doneness by seeing if the light skinlike covering on the tongue peels away easily. You want it to be tender but retain its shape rather than shredding when you slice it. Keep cooking until it reaches this temperature and consistency. Alternatively, if you have a slow cooker, it's a great way to cook a tongue. You can cook it on the low setting overnight, and in the morning (after 8 to 10 hours), it will be perfect.
2. When the tongue is done, remove it from the cooking water and let it cool on a plate or baking sheet. Reserve the liquid in which the tongue has cooked, since it makes a rich and savory base for picadillo. Once cool, freeze to use later.
3. Peel away the tongue's skinlike covering and the rough patch beneath the tongue, where it was attached. Slice the tongue crosswise into ¼-inch / 6mm-wide slices.
4. In a large skillet over medium-high heat, heat the oil until it's shimmering. Add the onion and sauté until it's translucent but not browned. Add the salsa and bring it to a simmer. Add the sliced tongue and stir until it's coated and hot. If you didn't overcook the tongue, it won't fall apart. (Even if you did, it will still taste great.)
5. Serve over rice or use as a filling for tacos or tortas. Store leftovers in a sealed container in the refrigerator for up to 3 days. To reheat, warm in a saucepan over low heat.

Meatballs With Morita Chile Sauce

Prep time: 5 minutes | Cook time: 35 minutes| Serves 6

- MEATBALLS
- 1 lb / 455g ground beef
- 1 lb / 455g ground pork
- 5 oz / 140g chicharrones, ground with a mortar and pestle or finely chopped
- ¾ cup / 90g minced onions
- 2 eggs
- 2 garlic cloves, chopped
- ½ cup / 10g parsley leaves, chopped
- ½ tsp sea salt
- 2 Tbsp olive oil
- Salsa de Chile Morita for Meatballs
- 1½ cups / 360ml vegetable oil
- 2 dried moritas chiles
- 8 Roma tomatoes, cored
- 1 white onion, chopped
- 1 garlic clove, chopped
- 1 Tbsp sea salt
- Pinch of freshly ground black pepper
- 1 tsp dried oregano
- ½ cup / 120ml olive oil

1. To make the meatballs: In a large bowl, combine the ground beef and pork, chicharrones, onion, eggs, garlic, parsley, and salt until well combined. Form the mixture into 2½-inch / 6cm balls.
2. Line a plate with a brown paper bag. Heat the olive oil in a skillet over medium-high heat. Once it's shimmering, gently drop the meatballs into the skillet and sear them on all sides, just to get them browned (but not cooked all the way through). If needed, do this in batches. Once seared, remove them from the oil and place them on the plate while you prepare the salsa.
3. To make the salsa: Pour the vegetable oil into a Dutch oven or other heavy-bottom pot over high heat. Fry the chiles, with their stems still on, for 1 to 2 minutes. As soon as they puff up, remove them from the oil (but keep the oil in the pan and turn off the heat). Once they're cool enough to handle, remove their stems and shake out and discard their seeds. Place the fried chiles in the jar of a blender.
4. Place the tomatoes in the same pot with the oil in which you fried the chiles and cook over medium-high heat, until their skins brown and they slump. Carefully transfer them with the slotted spoon to the jar of the blender with the chiles.
5. Add the onion and garlic to the pot and sauté until translucent, pour them and the remaining oil from the pot into the blender. Add the salt, pepper, oregano, and olive oil and puree everything together.
6. Pour the blended sauce into your Dutch oven or pot. Bring it to a boil over medium-high heat, then decrease to a simmer. Add the seared meatballs and simmer for about 20 minutes.
7. The meatballs can be stored in a sealed container in the refrigerator for up to 4 days.

Charred Sweet Potatoes with Black Salsa and Roasted Bone Marrow

Prep time: 5 minutes | Cook time: 65 minutes| Serves 6

- ½ cup / 130g sea salt
- 2 or 3 large orange-fleshed sweet potatoes
- 4 pasture-raised beef femur bones, split lengthwise
- 1 recipe Black Salsa
- 1 recipe "Fierce" Salsa
- 1 recipe Corn Tortillas, warmed
- Lime wedges

1. Preheat the oven to 425°F / 220°C.
2. Sprinkle ¼ cup / 65g of the sea salt on a plate. Wash the sweet potatoes well. While their skins are wet, roll them in the sea salt so they are as encrusted with salt as possible. Place them on a baking sheet, prick each one a few times with a fork, and bake for 50 to 55 minutes, until tender. Remove from the oven and let them cool while you roast your bones.
3. Sprinkle the remaining ¼ cup / 65g salt across the cut surfaces of the bones. It may seem like a lot, but this salt is what will bring out the meaty flavor of the roasting marrow. Roast the bones in the oven for 20 minutes, until well browned.
4. In the last 5 minutes before the bones come out of the oven, char the skin of each of your roasted sweet potatoes, holding them with tongs directly over the flame of your stove top burner and rotating them to char as much of the surface area as possible. You could also do this by placing the sweet potatoes directly on the coals of a grill. The goal is for the skins to get really blackened, but if you can't do this at home (if you have an electric stove, for example), this dish will still taste great even without the char.
5. Split the sweet potatoes in half lengthwise and place half on each plate, along with one roasted bone half. Place bowls of salsa negra and salsa brava on the table and pass a basket of warm tortillas so guests can scoop out the bone marrow, spread some on their tortilla, and top with a dollop of sweet potato and salsa. A few slivers of onion from the salsa brava add a delightful crunch and tang, in contrast to the potato's sweetness, and a squeeze of lime unites the flavors.

Baked Rice and Ground Beef Casserole

Prep time: 5 minutes | Cook time: 35 minutes| Serves 8

- ¼ cup / 55g unsalted butter
- Rice
- 1 qt / 960ml water
- ½ white onion, sliced
- 3 garlic cloves
- 2 jalapeños
- 1½ tsp saffron
- 1 tsp sea salt
- 2 cups / 400g white rice (preferably medium grain)
- Picadillo
- 2 Tbsp safflower oil
- ½ white onion, chopped
- ½ large red bell pepper, chopped
- 1 lb / 455g ground beef or pork or a combination of the two
- Healthy pinch of freshly ground black pepper
- Pinch of ground cloves
- Pinch of ground cinnamon
- 1 Tbsp raisins, coarsely chopped
- 2 Tbsp slivered almonds
- 1 garlic clove, chopped
- 4 or 5 Roma tomatoes, cored and chopped
- 1 Tbsp coarsely chopped parsley leaves
- ⅓ cup / 40g chopped olives (preferably Castelvetrano)
- 1 Tbsp capers, chopped
- 2 Tbsp sweet sherry
- 2 Tbsp apple cider vinegar
- 1 tsp sea salt, plus more as needed
- ½ cup / 100g granulated sugar
- 7 eggs

1. Preheat the oven to 375°F / 190°C.
2. Use the full ¼ cup / 55g of butter to thoroughly coat the base and sides of a 9 x 13-inch / 23 x 33cm baking dish. This will help form the crust.
3. To make the rice: In a 4- to 6-qt / 3.8 to 5.7L Dutch oven or other heavy-bottom pot, combine the water, onion, garlic, jalapeños, saffron, and salt. Bring to a boil over high heat, add the rice, and cover. When the water returns to a boil, decrease the heat so that it barely simmers. Cover and cook for 18 to 20 minutes. Then remove the lid and discard the jalapeños, onion, garlic, and whatever saffron threads may have settled on top of the rice, so that only the rice remains. Gently fluff the rice with a fork and set aside to cool.
4. While the rice is cooling, make the picadillo: Heat the oil in a large skillet over medium-high heat until it's hot but not smoking. Add the onion and bell pepper and sauté until soft, about 5 minutes. Add the ground meat and break it up with a wooden spoon as it cooks. Once it has browned, add the black pepper, cloves, cinnamon, raisins, almonds, garlic, tomatoes, parsley, olives, capers, sherry, vinegar, and salt. Keep cooking, stirring frequently, until all of the liquid has been absorbed, 10 to 12 minutes. Taste and add more salt if needed.

5. In a large bowl, combine ¼ cup / 50g of the sugar and the eggs and whisk well. Pour the cooled rice into the bowl and combine with the eggs and sugar. Spoon half of this rice-egg mixture into the buttered casserole dish and press down. Bake for 15 minutes, until the top is set. Remove from the oven and spread the picadillo mixture over the crust of rice. Pour the remaining rice-egg mixture on top of the picadillo and spread evenly, using a spatula. Sprinkle the remaining ¼ cup / 50g sugar on top.
6. Return to the oven and bake for 7 to 9 minutes, until the top is just turning golden brown. If you want it darker, you can broil it for the final 1 to 2 minutes. Let it cool for 5 minutes before cutting into squares and serving.
7. Store in a sealed container in the refrigerator for up to 3 days.

Shredded Steak Salad

Prep time: 5 minutes | Cook time: 45 minutes| Serves 6

- 2 lb / 910g flank steak
- 2 qt / 2L water
- 2 bay leaves (preferably fresh)
- 2 garlic cloves
- 2 Tbsp sea salt
- 2 heads romaine lettuce, washed and finely chopped
- 1 large or 2 small tomatoes, cored and finely chopped
- 6 radishes, thinly sliced
- 2 Tbsp minced white onion
- ½ cup / 120ml extra-virgin olive oil
- ¼ cup / 60ml champagne vinegar or sherry vinegar
- 1 tsp dried oregano
- Juice of 1 lime
- 1 tsp Maldon sea salt or another finishing salt, plus more as needed
- 2 avocados, cut in half, pitted, peeled, and cut into ½-inch / 12mm chunks

1. In a Dutch oven or a stockpot, cover the flank steak with the water and add the bay leaves and garlic. Bring to a boil, then decrease the heat and let it simmer for 1½ hours. Add the salt and cook 30 minutes more, until the meat is tender enough to shred easily. Once the steak is tender, let it cool in the water until you can handle it. Then remove the meat from the broth (cool and freeze this broth for another purpose) and shred it.
2. In a large salad bowl, toss the shredded steak with the romaine, tomato, radishes, and onion.
3. In a small bowl, whisk together the oil, vinegar, oregano, and lime juice. Pour the vinaigrette over the salad and season with the finishing salt. Toss to coat everything well. Taste and add more finishing salt if needed. Add the avocados and toss gently, so that they don't get mashed. Serve immediately.

Steak Tacos with Tomatillo Sauce

Prep time: 5 minutes | Cook time: 35 minutes| Serves 4

- 1 tablespoon olive or canola oil
- 8 ounces (225 g) white mushrooms, thinly sliced
- 1 medium tomato, seeded and diced
- ½ green bell pepper, diced
- 1 pound (455 g) lean round steak, excess fat trimmed, thinly sliced
- 1 cup (240 ml) Roasted Tomatillo Sauce, plus more for serving
- ½ teaspoon salt
- ½ teaspoon black pepper, or to taste
- Corn tortillas
- ½ cup (120 g) low-fat plain Greek yogurt

1. Heat the oil in a large nonstick skillet over medium heat. Sauté the mushrooms, tomato, and bell pepper until tender, 5 to 7 minutes. Transfer to a plate and set aside.
2. In the same skillet, sauté the beef over medium-high heat until browned, 7 to 10 minutes. Add the cooked vegetables, then the tomatillo sauce, salt, and black pepper. Cover and simmer for 20 minutes, to allow the flavors to blend.
3. Warm the tortillas on a griddle or large skillet. Keep warm.
4. When ready to serve, divide the meat and vegetable mixture among the tortillas. Serve with a dollop of the yogurt and top with extra tomatillo sauce, if desired.

Spicy Braised Beef

Prep time: 5 minutes | Cook time: 55 minutes| Serves 8

- 3 large tomatoes, chopped
- 1 small onion, chopped
- ½ green bell pepper, seeded and chopped
- 3 garlic cloves, chopped
- 1 teaspoon salt
- ½ teaspoon chili powder
- ½ teaspoon ground cumin
- ⅛ teaspoon dried Mexican oregano
- 3 pounds (1.3 kg) lean round steak, excess fat trimmed, cut into 1-inch (2.5 cm) pieces

1. Place the tomatoes, onion, pepper, garlic, salt, chili powder, cumin, and oregano in a blender or food processor and blend until smooth. Set aside.
2. Place the steak in a Dutch oven or large pot over medium-high heat and cook until browned, 7 to 10 minutes, then drain the excess fat. Add the vegetable mixture and bring to a boil. Reduce the heat, cover, and simmer until the meat is tender, about 45 minutes.

Sea Bass, Purslane, and Cactus with Salsa Verde

Prep time: 5 minutes | Cook time: 55 minutes| Serves 6

- SALSA VERDE WITH PURSLANE
- 1 lb / 455g small tomatillos, papery husks removed and discarded, rinsed
- 1 large white onion, cut in half, half left intact and the other half chopped
- 2 garlic cloves
- 3 or 4 serrano chiles, stemmed, seeded, and veins removed (or not, depending on how spicy you want this to be)
- 1 tsp sea salt
- Pinch of freshly ground black pepper
- 3 Tbsp / 45ml vegetable oil
- 1 lb / 910g purslane, well rinsed and leaves cut from the stems
- 4 to 6 cactus paddles, dethorned
- Olive oil
- 4 to 6 (6 oz / 170g) sea bass fillets
- 1 tsp sea salt
- Generous pinch of freshly ground black pepper
- 1 recipe Refried Beans

1. To make the salsa: Begin by placing the tomatillos in a Dutch oven or heavy-bottom skillet, together with the half intact onion, garlic, and serranos. Add enough water just to cover and bring to a boil. Decrease the heat and simmer for 10 minutes. Pour the contents of the Dutch oven into the jar of a blender, add the salt and pepper, and liquefy.
2. Warm the vegetable oil in a large skillet over medium heat. Add the chopped onion and sauté until it's translucent but not browned. Then add the salsa from the blender and simmer for 10 minutes. In the last minute, add the purslane and stir to combine and heat through.
3. While your salsa is simmering, grill your cactus paddles. Heat a grill to medium or a grill pan over medium-high heat. Score the cactus paddles by slicing thin crosshatched lines across each flat surface. Rub them with the olive oil to keep them from sticking and then place them on the hot grill or grill pan, and cook for 6 to 7 minutes on each side. Place the grilled cactus on the bottom of a baking dish large enough to accommodate them.
4. Preheat the oven to 350°F / 180°C.
5. Arrange the sea bass fillets on top of the grilled cactus. Season with the salt and pepper. Cover with the salsa and bake for 25 to 30 minutes.
6. Serve hot, with the refried beans.

Noodles with Seafood

Prep time: 5 minutes | Cook time: 45 minutes| Serves 6

- OCTOPUS
- 1 (2 to 2½ lb / 910g to 1.2 kg) fresh or thawed frozen whole octopus, rinsed
- 4 scallions, crowns discarded
- 1 tomato, punctured with the tines of a fork (so that it doesn't explode in the pot)
- 1 garlic clove
- 2 bay leaves (preferably fresh)
- 4 sprigs thyme
- ¼ cup / 65g sea salt
- 3 cups / 720ml Fish Stock
- 3 or 4 Roma tomatoes, cored
- 1 garlic clove
- ½ white onion
- 1 tsp sea salt
- 2 Tbsp safflower oil
- 7 oz / 200g angel hair pasta
- 12 steamed clams
- 6 oz / 120g shrimp, shelled and deveined
- 1 lime, cut in half
- 1 recipe Chipotle Mayonnaise

1. Begin by cooking your octopus: Put the octopus, scallions, tomato, garlic, bay leaves, thyme, and salt in a large stockpot and add water to cover by about 2 inches / 5cm. Bring to a boil, then decrease the heat and simmer with the lid on for 2 hours. If using a pressure cooker, cook under high pressure for 20 minutes. Once the octopus is cooked, it will have shrunk to about 50 percent of its original size and will puncture easily, since the flesh will be tender. The skin should come off easily but the suckers less so.
2. Remove the octopus from the pot and let it cool until you can handle it. Starting with the tentacles, pull off any loose skin, which should slip off like a sock, and discard. You don't need to worry about getting all of it off, just the parts that come off easily. Chop the body and tentacles into bite-size pieces and set them aside.
3. In the jar of a blender, combine the stock, tomatoes, garlic, onion, and salt and liquefy.
4. In a Dutch oven or heavy-bottom saucepan over medium heat, warm the oil until it's shimmering but not smoking. Add the pasta, breaking the noodles into 2-inch / 5cm lengths as you drop them into the hot oil. With a wooden spoon or spatula, stir them continuously as they fry to a golden color. Pour the contents of the blender over the fried noodles. Bring to a simmer and continue to cook until the noodles are very soft and most of the liquid is absorbed, about 8 minutes. Don't worry if it's still a bit soupy. This is a wet casserole, and more of the moisture will cook out in the final broiling step.
5. Preheat the broiler.
6. Pour the cooked noodles and their sauce into a paella dish or a large, shallow casserole dish. Tuck the chunks of cooked octopus, the steamed clams, and the raw shrimp into the top of the noodles. You could also use steamed mussels or other seafood if you prefer—it all tastes delicious. Broil for 3 to 4 minutes, until the top is just crusty and a little browned.
7. Finish with a squeeze of lime, a dollop of mayonnaise, and a scattering of parsley and serve immediately.

Chicken Or Pork In Green Mole

Prep time: 5 minutes | Cook time: 45 minutes| Serves 6

- 2 Tbsp olive oil
- 1½ lb / 650g skin-on chicken thighs or boneless pork shoulder, cut into 1- to 2-inch / 2.5 to 5cm cubes
- 2½ cups / 300g pumpkin seeds
- 1 white onion, quartered
- 2 garlic cloves
- 4 serrano chiles, stemmed, seeded, and veins removed (or not, depending on how spicy you want this to be)
- 6 cups / 1.4L Chicken Stock
- 2 cups / 40g cilantro stems and leaves
- 2 lb / 910g green beans, cut into 1-inch / 2.5cm pieces
- 2 Tbsp sea salt, plus more as needed
- 1 recipe cooked egg noodles

1. Warm the oil in a large skillet over medium-high heat. Once the oil is shimmering, sear the chicken or pork in batches, being careful not to crowd the pan. (Normally you salt meat when you sear it, but you don't want to salt a green mole until the last minute because salt can cause it to turn watery.) Sear the meat on all sides, until it is noticeably browned but not cooked through. Transfer the seared meat to a plate and set it aside while you make the sauce.
2. In a dry skillet over medium-high heat, toast the pumpkin seeds until they turn golden brown, being careful to stir them regularly so they don't burn.
3. In the jar of a blender, grind the pumpkin seeds. Add the onion, garlic, and chiles and pulse to puree. Add 3 cups / 720ml of the stock with the cilantro, and pulse to liquefy. Pour the contents of the blender into a large Dutch oven or heavy-bottom pot and turn the heat to medium-low. Cook, stirring, until the sauce is simmering, about 15 minutes. Add the chicken or pork, cover the pot, and cook over low heat for about 45 minutes, until the sauce is thick and the meat is tender and beginning to fall apart. Add the green beans and the salt and cook for 10 to 15 minutes more. Taste and add more salt if needed.
4. Serve with the rice or over the egg noodles. The mole can be stored in a sealed container in the refrigerator for 3 to 5 days.

Mussel Tamales

Prep time: 5 minutes | Cook time: 45 minutes| Makes 10 to 12 tamales

- 1 package banana leaves
- 4 cups / 1kg fresh masa or 4 cups / 520g masa harina mixed with 2 to 2½ cups / 480 to 600ml water
- ¼ cup / 50g lard
- 2 Tbsp unsalted butter
- 2 tsp sea salt
- ½ cup / 10g parsley leaves, minced
- 1 Tbsp olive oil
- 1 leek, trimmed, cut in half lengthwise and thoroughly washed
- 36 large mussels or 50 smaller ones, well scrubbed so that no grit or beards remain

1. Cut your banana leaves into 24 place mat–size rectangles. Then run each one swiftly over the flame of your burner. You're not looking to toast them, but the heat of the fire loosens the fibers and makes the leaves more pliable.
2. In the bowl of a stand mixer fitted with the paddle attachment, combine the masa, lard, butter, and 1 tsp of the salt and beat on medium-high speed for 3 to 4 minutes, until it gets much fluffier. The more air you can whip into the masa, the better, since this keeps the tamales light-tasting. Fold in the parsley and lemon zest.
3. Oil a comal or skillet and heat it over medium-high heat. Sprinkle the remaining 1 tsp of salt on the cut side of the leek and place it cut-side down on the hot comal or skillet. Once it begins to soften, flip it over and cook the other side. When it has cooked through and looks translucent, take it off the stove and cut it into 1-inch / 2.5cm pieces.
4. Spread 2 heaping Tbsp of the masa mixture in the center of one of your prepped banana leaves, using the back of a spoon or a spatula to paint a rectangle about 3 inches / 7.5cm wide by 4 inches / 10cm long and ½ inch / 12mm thick.
5. Place as many mussels as fit over the strip of masa, followed by a few pieces of grilled leek. (Divide your leek so that each tamal gets an equal amount.)
6. Now it's time to fold the banana leaf. Don't worry that there isn't masa on top of the mussels and leeks. Once you fold it and it steams, it will all mix up. You just want to make sure that the mussels are well embedded in the masa. Fold the leaf around the mussels as if you were making an envelope or wrapping a package. Once it's wrapped, place the whole package facedown on top of another cut banana leaf and wrap that around the original package. Again, it isn't important exactly how you wrap it, just that it is completely wrapped up so that the masa doesn't ooze out in the steaming process. Repeat this process until you have packaged 10 to 12 tamales.
7. Place a few inches of water in the bottom of a steamer. Put all of the tamal packages in the steamer basket, not stacked in a single tower but arranged in layers of three or so, as flat as possible, with room for a little steam to rise in between them. Turn on the heat, cover the pot with a lid, and bring the water to a boil, then decrease it to a simmer. Steam the tamales for 20 to 25 minutes, monitoring about halfway through the process to make sure that there is still a good inch or two of water at the bottom of the pan and adding more water if necessary.
8. To check if the tamales are thoroughly cooked, open the top parcel and see if the masa is firm to the touch. It shouldn't be wet and soupy anymore. Try cutting into the center with a knife to ensure that the masa has the consistency of firm polenta and doesn't ooze at all. As soon as the tamales are ready, remove them from the heat and serve them while they're still hot. If you're not quite ready to eat them, you can keep them warm in the pot with the heat off and a lid on for up to 30 minutes.
9. While most tamales can be steamed, then refrigerated, and then steamed again, these are an exception, because the mussels should be eaten hot, shortly after they first open.

Pork and Chicken Posole

Prep time: 5 minutes | Cook time: 65 minutes| Serves 8

- 1 tablespoon olive oil
- 1 medium onion, finely chopped
- 2 garlic cloves, minced
- 1¼ pounds (565 g) chicken breast meat, cooked and shredded
- 4 ounces (115 g) pork tenderloin, cooked and shredded
- Two 29-ounce (822 g) cans white hominy, drained and rinsed (about 7 cups)
- ½ cup (120 ml) Mexican Spice Blend, or to taste
- 2 tablespoons chili powder
- 1½ teaspoons salt
- ¼ teaspoon dried Mexican oregano
- 2 tablespoons masa harina
- Thinly sliced radishes
- Shredded cabbage
- Chopped cilantro
- Lime wedges

1. Heat the oil in a Dutch oven or large pot over medium heat. Add the onion and sauté until translucent, 5 to 6 minutes. Add the garlic and sauté for 1 more minute.
2. Add the chicken and pork and warm slightly, about 5 minutes. Add the hominy, spice blend, chili powder, salt, oregano, and 7½ cups (1.8 L) water and stir to combine.
3. Bring to a boil, then reduce the heat, cover, and simmer for 30 minutes, until heated through and the flavors have blended. Taste and adjust seasonings.
4. Mix the masa harina and ½ cup (120 ml) water in a small bowl. Add to the pot and stir to prevent lumps from forming. Allow to simmer until the broth thickens slightly, about 20 minutes.
5. Serve with shredded cabbage, radishes, cilantro, and lime wedges.

Pork and Chicken Tamal

Prep time: 5 minutes | Cook time: about 6 hours | Serves 8

- ½ lb / 230g chicken breasts or thighs
- ½ lb / 230g boneless pork shoulder
- 2½ Tbsp sea salt
- 2 white onions, 1 left whole and 1 minced
- 1 bay leaf (preferably fresh)
- 2 cloves
- 1 avocado leaf
- ¼ cup / 5g epazote leaves, 1 large leaf left whole and the remainder minced
- 1 Tbsp achiote (annatto) seeds
- 2 Tbsp white vinegar
- 1 garlic clove
- 3 Roma tomatoes, 2 left whole and 1 cored and minced
- 1 cup / 240ml reserved pork/chicken cooking liquid
- 4 cups / 1kg fresh masa or 4 cups / 520g masa harina, mixed with 2 to 2½ cups / 480 to 600ml water
- 1 cup plus 2 Tbsp / 250g lard
- 1 package banana leaves, plus kitchen twine for binding
- 1 recipe Pickled Red Onions

1. To cook the meat: Place both meats in a slow cooker if you have one, and cover with at least 6 cups / 1.4L water plus 1 Tbsp of the salt, the whole onion, bay leaf, cloves, and avocado leaf. Cook at a very low simmer for 5 to 6 hours, until the meat is soft and stringy. If you are doing this in a heavy-bottom stockpot on the stove, I suggest beginning with the pork plus the water, salt, onion, and aromatics, simmering it for about 20 minutes, then adding the chicken for another 20 minutes. Once the meat is completely tender and falls apart when you prod it with a fork, turn off the stove and let the meat cool until you can handle it. Strain the meat from the cooking liquid, reserving the liquid and discarding the onion and aromatics.
2. In the jar of a blender, liquefy the whole epazote leaf, achiote, vinegar, garlic, the 2 whole Roma tomatoes, 1 Tbsp of the salt, and 1 cup / 240ml of the reserved liquid in which the meat cooked.
3. In the bowl of your stand mixer fitted with the paddle attachment (or in a very large bowl, using your hands), combine the liquid from the blender with the masa, the remaining ½ Tbsp salt, the minced onion, the minced tomato, the minced epazote, and 1 cup / 220g of the lard and mix on low speed. It will be a very liquidy, sticky mixture.
4. To prepare your banana leaves, run each one swiftly over the flame of your burner. You're not looking to toast them, but the heat of the fire loosens the fibers and makes the leaves more pliable. Spread a leaf with a 9-inch / 23cm pie-size circle of the masa mixture. Place the shredded meat in the center and then distribute an equal amount of the masa mixture on top of the meat to cover it. Wrap the large tamal with a banana leaf, then wrap it in another one and continue until the parcel is tightly enveloped. Use

your string to bind the parcel.
5. In order to steam your pibipollo, place a large steamer basket at the bottom of a heavy-bottom stockpot and add a few inches of water. Place the parcel in the basket, cover, and bring the water at the bottom of the pot to a slow boil over medium heat. Leave the lid on and steam for about 40 minutes. In the last 10 minutes of this steaming time, preheat the oven to 350°F / 180°C.
6. Once the tamal has steamed and the masa is no longer falling apart, place it on a baking sheet or in a casserole dish it can fit in. Partially unwrap the parcel so the top of the pibipollo is exposed. Dab the top with the remaining 2 Tbsp of the lard and put it in the oven for 10 minutes if it is still hot from being steamed, 20 minutes if it was cold. It's perfectly fine to steam the pibipollo ahead of time and do this last baking step right before serving.
7. Slice into your pibipollo as you would a pie and serve hot, with the pickled onions.

Slow Cooker Pork Pernil Tacos

Prep time: 5 minutes | Cook time: about 3 hours | Serves 12

- 3 pounds (1.3 kg) pork tenderloin
- 5 or 6 garlic cloves, crushed
- 1 cup (240 ml) fresh orange juice (from about 3 oranges)
- ¼ cup (60 ml) fresh lime juice
- 1½ teaspoons ground cumin
- 1½ teaspoons salt
- ½ teaspoon dried Mexican oregano
- ¼ teaspoon black pepper
- 24 corn tortillas
- Shredded lettuce
- Chopped tomatoes
- 1 cup (120 g) crumbled queso blanco

1. Use a sharp knife to cut four slits into the pork and place four of the garlic cloves into the holes. Place the pork in a large zipper bag.
2. Combine the remaining garlic, orange juice, lime juice, cumin, salt, oregano, and pepper in a small bowl. Pour over the pork and seal the bag. Allow to marinate in the refrigerator for at least 12 hours, turning once.
3. Remove the pork from the refrigerator and allow to stand for about 30 minutes. Transfer the pork along with the marinade to a slow cooker and cook on low for 4 to 6 hours, until the pork reaches an internal temperature of 145°F (60°C). Check the temperature after about 3 hours.
4. Remove the pork, shred using two forks, and return to the slow cooker with the cooking liquid. Warm for about 15 minutes.
5. Serve on warm corn tortillas with lettuce, tomatoes, and the queso blanco.

Red Mole From Tepoztlán

Prep time: 5 minutes | Cook time: about 2 hours | Serves 12

- 9 oz / 255g mulato chiles, stemmed and seeded
- Pinch of aniseeds
- Pinch of cumin seeds
- 2 black peppercorns
- 2 allspice berries
- 2 cloves
- ½ cinnamon stick
- 4 to 6 Tbsp / 50 to 75g lard
- 2 whole chickens, cut into serving-size pieces
- ¼ cup / 30g pine nuts
- 3 Tbsp / 30 g pumpkin seeds
- Scant ¼ cup / 30g black raisins
- 3 Tbsp / 30 g almonds
- ¼ cup / 30g hazelnuts
- 3 Tbsp / 30 g peanuts
- ¼ cup / 30g pecans
- 3 Tbsp / 30 g sesame seeds
- 6 Ritz or other rich-tasting crackers
- 1 corn tortilla
- 2 slices fluffy white bread (dinner roll or ciabatta)
- ½ white onion, coarsely chopped
- 2 Roma tomatoes, cored and quartered
- 1 very ripe (black) plantain, peeled and cut into chunks
- 1 large garlic clove
- 5 oz / 140g semisweet chocolate
- ¼ cup / 60ml water
- 6 cups / 1.4L Chicken Stock

1. First, lightly toast the chiles by placing them on a hot, ungreased comal or in a skillet over medium heat, turning them constantly as they heat up and begin to release their fragrance. Before they turn brown, remove them from the heat and submerge them in a bowl of water to let them soak and soften while you prepare everything else.

2. Next, you are going to toast all of the spices on your hot, dry comal or in an ungreased skillet. You should do this in batches because they have different toasting times, beginning with the ones that will toast the fastest: the anise and cumin. As soon as you can smell these toasted seeds, take them off the comal or skillet and place them in a spice grinder. Now do the same with the peppercorns, allspice, cloves, and cinnamon stick. After they're toasted, add them to your spice grinder and grind the spices together. Dump the ground spices into a large bowl. You will be frying things in batches that you will be adding to this bowl. Eventually, all of this will go into the blender, but for now, you need a place to store the mole ingredients as you prepare them to be blended together.

3. Now sear the chicken that you are going to cook in the sauce. Melt 4 Tbsp / 50g of the lard in a Dutch oven or large heavy-bottom skillet over medium-high heat. When the lard has melted completely and is shimmering, place as many pieces of the chicken in the pot as you can fit without crowding. The goal here is to brown each piece, so be sure they're not overlapping. Sprinkle them lightly with salt and flip them over so that both sides get seared. When they look golden, using tongs, transfer them to a platter and repeat with the rest of the chicken pieces, adding more lard to the pan as needed. The chicken should be just seared and not be cooked though at this stage because it will continue cooking in the mole sauce.

4. Once you're finished searing the chicken, keep whatever grease and drippings remain in the Dutch oven or skillet to fry other things. You want about ½ inch / 12mm of shimmering oil in the bottom of the pan, and you will have to add more lard as needed. You are going to be frying the nuts and seeds in batches because, depending on their sizes, they will cook at different rates. You are looking for each thing to turn golden but not dark brown.

5. Begin with the pine nuts, pumpkin seeds, and raisins. Once you can smell the fragrance of these nuts and seeds and they look golden, remove them with a slotted spoon and place them in the big bowl with the spices. Now fry the almonds, hazelnuts, peanuts, and pecans until they are fragrant and golden and then add them to the big bowl. Fry the sesame seeds by themselves, being extra careful to monitor them the whole time and moving them around with a wooden spoon or spatula as they fry because they can burn quickly. Add the sesame seeds to the big bowl.

6. Remember to add more lard to the pan when you need it, since the nuts and seeds will likely have soaked it up. Once the added lard has melted and is shimmering, fry the Ritz crackers very briefly, because they burn fast, then the tortilla, and finally the bread, placing it all in the big bowl with all of the previously toasted and fried ingredients. Add more lard if needed and fry the onion, tomatoes, plantain, and garlic until everything is golden and a bit stewy, then add it all to the big bowl.

7. In a small saucepot, combine the chocolate with the water and heat until the chocolate melts. Turn off the heat while you blend your sauce ingredients.

8. Due to the amount of volume here, you are going to need to blend your sauce in batches. Know that from this point on, everything is getting blended together and then simmered, so the order in which you blend things doesn't much matter. You want a ratio of about 1:1 of stock to solid ingredients. I would suggest blending a couple of cups of solids at a time (4 cups / 960ml total, including the stock). When the contents of the blender are liquefied, dump it into your largest stockpot and then repeat the process. Finally, blend the soaked chiles with the remaining stock and add this to your pot, along with the melted chocolate, and stir well to combine.

9. Bring the mole to a simmer over medium-low heat. Drop the chicken into the pot and cover. Let it simmer for 20 to 25 minutes, then serve. The mole can be stored in a sealed container in the refrigerator for 3 to 4 days or frozen for up to 3 months.

Mexican Cod Steaks

Prep time: 5 minutes | Cook time: 25 minutes| Serves 4

- 1 tablespoon olive oil
- 1 green bell pepper, thinly sliced
- 1 red bell pepper, thinly sliced
- 1 large onion, thinly sliced
- 2 tablespoons Mexican Spice Blend
- 2 garlic cloves, crushed
- ½ teaspoon salt
- 4 cod fillets, about 4 ounces (115 g) each

1. Heat the oil in a large nonstick skillet over medium heat. Add the peppers and onion, followed by the spice blend, garlic, and salt, and sauté, stirring frequently, until the onion is translucent, 5 to 7 minutes. Remove from the pan and set aside. Do not wipe out the skillet.
2. Place the cod in the skillet, then arrange the vegetables on top. Cover and cook until the fish is opaque and flaky, 10 to 15 minutes.

Swordfish Steaks with Salsa

Prep time: 5 minutes | Cook time: 15 minutes| Serves 4

- 2 tablespoons olive oil
- ½ cup (60 g) chopped onion
- 2 garlic cloves, crushed
- 4 swordfish steaks, approximately 4 ounces (115 g) each
- 1 jalapeño, stemmed, seeded, and finely chopped
- 5 medium tomatoes, seeded and finely chopped
- ½ cup (20 g) chopped cilantro
- 1 tablespoon fresh lime juice

1. Heat 1 tablespoon of the oil in a large skillet over medium-high heat. Sauté the onion until translucent, about 5 minutes, then add the garlic and sauté for 1 more minute. Remove from the skillet and set aside.
2. Heat the remaining 1 tablespoon oil in the skillet, then add the swordfish and cook for 2 to 3 minutes on each side. The swordfish flesh should become opaque and flake easily. Remove from the skillet and keep warm.
3. Sauté the jalapeño in the skillet until tender, 2 to 3 minutes. Add the tomatoes, cilantro, and lime juice and continue to sauté, stirring frequently, until the tomatoes have softened, about 5 minutes. Add the garlic and onion and stir to combine. Spoon over the fish and serve.

Red Snapper In Tomatillo Sauce

Prep time: 5 minutes | Cook time: 15 minutes| Serves 8

- 2 pounds (910 g) red snapper fillets
- ½ teaspoon salt
- Black pepper
- 2 limes, thinly sliced
- 2 teaspoons olive oil
- 1 cup (240 ml) Roasted Tomatillo Sauce

1. Line a baking sheet with foil. Place the fish on the baking sheet and sprinkle with the salt and pepper. Place the lime slices on the fillets. Cover with foil and refrigerate for 4 to 5 hours.
2. Preheat the oven to 400°F (200°C).
3. Brush the fillets with the oil. Bake for 30 minutes, or until the flesh turns opaque and flakes easily. Serve immediately with the tomatillo sauce.

Mexican Salmon Cakes

Prep time: 5 minutes | Cook time: 5 minutes| Serves 2

- ½ cup (70 g) plain bread crumbs
- Grated zest of 1 lemon
- ½ teaspoon salt
- ½ teaspoon black pepper
- One 7.5-ounce (213 g) can pink salmon, drained, broken into bite-sized pieces
- 1 egg
- ¼ cup (40 g) minced onion
- ¼ cup (35 g) minced red bell pepper
- 1 tablespoon olive oil

1. Mix the bread crumbs, lemon zest, salt, and black pepper in a medium bowl. Add the salmon, egg, onion, and bell pepper and stir to combine. Divide the mixture into four patties.
2. Heat the oil in a large nonstick skillet over medium-high heat. Cook the patties for 4 to 5 minutes on each side, until they are golden brown.

Grilled Chipotle Salmon

Prep time: 5 minutes | Cook time: 5 minutes| Serves 2

- Two 5-ounce (140 g) skin-on salmon steaks, about 1 inch (2.5 cm) thick
- ¼ cup (60 ml) fresh lime juice
- Nonstick cooking spray
- ½ cup (120 ml) no-salt-added tomato sauce
- ½ to 1 chipotle chile in adobo, or to taste
- ½ teaspoon salt
- ⅛ teaspoon black pepper

1. Place the salmon, skin side down, in a covered container with the lime juice. Place in the refrigerator to marinate for 1½ hours. Remove from the refrigerator and allow to come to room temperature before baking.
2. Preheat the oven to 350°F (180°C). Line a baking sheet with foil and spray with cooking spray.
3. Combine the tomato sauce and chipotle chile in adobo in a blender or food processor and blend until smooth.
4. Place the salmon, skin side down, on the baking sheet and season with the salt and pepper. Bake for about 20 minutes, until the thickest part of the salmon reaches 145°F (60°C). Serve with the chipotle sauce.

Fish Tacos with Cilantro Slaw

Prep time: 5 minutes | Cook time: 10 minutes| Serves 8

- CILANTRO SLAW
- ¼ cup (60 ml) extra virgin olive oil
- ¼ cup (60 ml) apple cider vinegar
- 1 tablespoon grated orange zest
- 2 tablespoons fresh orange juice
- 1 teaspoon sugar
- ½ teaspoon ground cumin
- ½ teaspoon salt
- Black pepper, to taste
- 2 cups (110 g) angel hair coleslaw mix
- ½ red bell pepper, finely chopped
- 1 cup (40 g) chopped cilantro
- FISH
- 2 pounds (910 g) red snapper, tilapia, or other white fish fillets
- 2 teaspoons ancho chile powder
- 1 teaspoon salt
- Black pepper
- 2 tablespoons olive oil
- To serve
- 16 corn tortillas
- Chopped cilantro
- Lime wedges

1. To make the slaw, combine the oil, vinegar, orange zest and juice, sugar, cumin, salt, and black pepper in a jar with a lid. Shake to mix and set aside.
2. Combine the coleslaw mix, bell pepper, and cilantro in a medium bowl. Add the vinegar dressing and mix well. Refrigerate until ready to serve.
3. To make the fish, heat an electric griddle to 350°F (180°C) or heat a large skillet over medium-high heat.
4. Season the fish fillets with the chile powder, salt, and black pepper on both sides.
5. Heat the oil on the griddle and panfry the fish to form a nice crust, 3 to 4 minutes on each side, until the fish is opaque and flakes easily. Set aside.
6. Heat the tortillas on the griddle for 2 to 3 minutes on each side. Transfer to a tortilla warmer or a clean kitchen towel to keep warm.
7. Just before serving, flake the fish and place on the tortillas. Top with the slaw and more cilantro. Serve with lime wedges.

Chapter 10
Drinks

Hibiscus Cooler

Prep time: 5 minutes | Cook time: 10 minutes | Serves 8 OR 2 QT / 2L

- 6 cups / 1.4L water
- 1½ oz / 40g organic dried hibiscus flowers
- 1 cinnamon stick
- ½ cup / 100g granulated sugar, plus more as needed
- 3 cups / 330g ice

1. In a medium saucepan over medium-high heat, bring 5 cups / 1.2L of the water to a boil. Decrease the heat to low and, when at a simmer, add the hibiscus and cinnamon stick. Simmer for about 20 minutes. Once it's done, the flowers will all have settled on the bottom of the pot. Pour the mixture through a fine-mesh strainer into a bowl, discarding the flowers, and place it in the refrigerator to cool it down.
2. Once you're ready to serve it, stir the sugar and the remaining 1 cup / 240ml water into the concentrate. Taste and stir in more sugar if needed.
3. Fill a serving pitcher or glasses with the ice and then pour the agua fresca over the ice.
4. The agua fresca can be stored in a glass container (it tastes better when stored in glass than in plastic, and it has the tendency to stain plastic) in the refrigerator for 2 or 3 days.

Whole Limeade

Prep time: 5 minutes | Cook time: 5 minutes | Serves 8 OR 2 QT / 2L

- 2 cups / 230g ice
- 6 cups / 1.4L water
- 2 whole organic seedless limes (or, if not seedless, then cut in half and seeded)
- ½ cup / 100g granulated sugar, plus more as needed

1. Place the ice and 2 cups / 480ml of the water in your serving pitcher.
2. Place the limes (skin and all) in the jar of a blender, making sure not to include any seeds, and add the remaining 4 cups / 960ml of the water and the sugar. Blend briefly by pulsing a few times. Taste and stir in more sugar if needed.
3. Pour the mixture over a fine-mesh strainer into the serving pitcher. Chill until ready to serve.
4. The agua fresca can be stored in the pitcher the refrigerator for 2 or 3 days.

Grapefruit-Ginger Drink

Prep time: 5 minutes | Cook time: 5 minutes | Serves 8 OR 2 QT / 2L

- 2 cups / 230g ice
- 6 cups / 1.4L water
- 1½ oz / 40g ginger, peeled and cut into rounds
- ½ cup / 100g granulated sugar, plus more as needed
- 1½ cups / 360ml freshly squeezed grapefruit juice

1. Place the ice and 2 cups / 480ml of the water in your serving pitcher.
2. Place the ginger, remaining 4 cups / 960ml of the water, sugar, and grapefruit juice in the jar of a blender and blend on high speed, until well blended. Taste and stir in more sugar if needed.
3. Pour the mixture over a fine-mesh strainer into the serving pitcher. Chill until ready to serve.
4. The agua fresca can be stored in the pitcher in the refrigerator for 2 or 3 days.

Cucumber and Mint Limeade

Prep time: 5 minutes | Cook time: 5 minutes | Serves 8 OR 2 QT / 2L

- 2 cups / 230g ice
- 6 cups / 1.4L water
- 10 to 20 mint leaves, plus 1 sprig, well washed
- ¼ cup / 60ml freshly squeezed lime juice
- ⅛ to ¼ English cucumber, peeled and 3 thin slices cut and reserved
- ½ cup / 100g granulated sugar, plus more as needed

1. Place the ice and 2 cups / 480ml of the water in your serving pitcher.
2. Place the mint leaves in the jar of a blender with the lime juice, cucumber, sugar, and the remaining 4 cups / 960ml of the water and blend completely. Taste and stir in more sugar if needed.
3. Pour the mixture over a fine-mesh strainer into the serving pitcher. Chill. Garnish with the sprig of mint and/or float the slices of cucumber on top and serve.
4. The agua fresca can be stored in the pitcher in the refrigerator for 2 or 3 days.

Beer with Lime and Salt

Prep time: 5 minutes | Cook time: 5 minutes | MAKES 1 COCKTAIL

- 1 Tbsp kosher salt
- ¼ lime
- 2 oz / 60ml freshly squeezed lime juice
- Bohemia or other Mexican beer, very cold

1. Spread the salt on a saucer. Rub the rim of a well-chilled beer stein or similar-size glass with the lime quarter and then dip the rim of the glass in the salt to coat.
2. Pour the lime juice into the bottom of the prepared glass and fill to the rim with ice cold beer.

Spicy Tomato Citrus Drink

Prep time: 5 minutes | Cook time: 5 minutes| MAKES 4½ CUPS / 1L PLUS 65ML

- 13 oz / 390ml tomato juice (this is a bit more than 1½ cups / 360ml)
- 13 oz / 390ml Clamato
- 3 oz / 90ml freshly squeezed lime juice
- 3 oz / 90ml freshly squeezed orange juice
- 4 oz / 120ml ketchup
- 1 Tbsp minced onion
- 1 Tbsp minced serrano chile
- 1 Tbsp minced cilantro leaves
- 1 Tbsp minced celery

1. In a large serving pitcher that you can chill, combine the tomato juice, Clamato, lime juice, orange juice, ketchup, onion, chile, cilantro, and celery. Refrigerate until cold. Store in the pitcher in the refrigerator for up to 2 days.

Pear and Pink Peppercorn Drink

Prep time: 5 minutes | Cook time: 5 minutes| Serves 8 OR 2 QT / 2L

- 2 cups / 230g ice
- 6 cups / 1.4L water
- 2 pears, stemmed, cored, and peeled
- 2 Tbsp freshly squeezed lemon juice
- ¼ cup / 50g granulated sugar, plus more if needed
- 2 pinches of pink peppercorns, plus more for garnish

1. Place the ice and 2 cups / 480ml of the water in your serving pitcher.
2. Place the pears, lemon juice, sugar, 1 pinch of the peppercorns, and the remaining 4 cups / 960ml of the water in the jar of a blender and blend on high speed, until well blended. Taste and stir in more sugar if needed.
3. Pour the mixture over a fine-mesh strainer into the serving pitcher. Chill. Float the remaining peppercorns on the surface and serve.
4. The agua fresca can be stored in the pitcher in the refrigerator for 2 or 3 days.

Blended Melon Drink

Prep time: 5 minutes | Cook time: 5 minutes| Serves 8 OR 1½ QT / 1.4L

- 2 cups / 230g ice
- 6 cups / 1.4L water
- Seeds of 1 cantaloupe or honeydew melon
- Flesh of ½ cantaloupe or honeydew melon
- ¼ cup / 50g granulated sugar, plus more as needed

1. Place the ice and 2 cups / 480ml of the water in your serving pitcher.
2. Place the seeds and flesh of the cantaloupe, the remaining 4 cups / 960ml of the water, and sugar into the jar of a blender and blend on high until well blended. Pour the mixture over a fine-mesh strainer into your serving pitcher, pressing on the solids to express all the liquid. Depending on how powerful your blender is, you may wish to repeat this process, returning the liquid to the blender and then straining it several times more to filter out as much of the grit as possible, so that all you're left with is a creamy, watery drink. Once you're satisfied with the texture, stir and taste. Add more sugar if needed. Serve the horchata over ice.
3. The horchata can be stored in the pitcher the refrigerator for 2 or 3 days. Separation is normal. Just stir the horchata until it becomes uniform and creamy again before serving.

Pineapple, Orange, and Basil Drink

Prep time: 5 minutes | **Cook time:** 10 minutes | **Serves 8 OR 2 QT / 2L**

- 2 cups / 230g ice
- 6 cups / 1.4L water
- ¼ pineapple, cut into pieces
- 1 orange, peeled
- ¼ cup / 50g granulated sugar, plus more as needed
- 3 to 4 fresh basil leaves (optional)

1. Place the ice and 2 cups / 480ml of the water in your serving pitcher.
2. Place the pineapple, orange, sugar, and the remaining 4 cups / 960ml of the water in the jar of a blender and blend on high until well blended. Add the basil and pulse until completely integrated and no small pieces remain. Taste and stir in more sugar if needed.
3. Pour the mixture over a fine-mesh strainer into the serving pitcher. Chill until ready to serve.
4. The agua fresca can be stored in the pitcher in the refrigerator for 2 or 3 days.

Blended Rice and Almond Drink

Prep time: 5 minutes | **Cook time:** 5 minutes | **Serves 8 OR 1½ QT / 1.4L**

- 1 cup / 200g jasmine rice
- ½ cup / 70g almonds
- 2 cinnamon sticks
- 1 pinch of cardamom or 1 whole pod
- 1 vanilla bean, split lengthwise, or 1 tsp vanilla extract
- 1½ qt / 1.4L water
- ½ cup / 100g granulated sugar, plus more as needed
- 2 cups / 230g ice

1. The night before you want to serve your horchata, cover the rice, almonds, cinnamon sticks, cardamom, and vanilla bean (or add the extract) with 3 cups / 720ml of the water and let soak overnight or for at least 8 hours in the refrigerator.
2. The next day, scrape the seeds from the soaked vanilla bean into the jar of a blender and discard the pod. Add the entire rice mixture, including the cinnamon sticks and cardamom pod, if using, and puree for about 3 minutes, until completely smooth.
3. Pour the mixture over a fine-mesh strainer into your serving pitcher, pressing on the solids to express all the liquid. Depending on how powerful your blender is, you may wish to repeat this process, returning the liquid to the blender and then straining it once more to filter out as much of the grit as possible, so that all you're left with is a creamy horchata. Once you're satisfied with the texture of your drink, add the sugar, the remaining 3 cups / 720ml of the water, and ice. Stir and taste. Add more sugar if needed. Serve the horchata over ice.
4. The horchata can be stored in the pitcher in the refrigerator for 2 to 3 days. Separation is normal. Just stir the horchata until it becomes uniform and creamy again before serving.

Mezcal Margarita

Prep time: 5 minutes | **Cook time:** 15 minutes | **MAKES 1 COCKTAIL**

- SIMPLE SYRUP
- 1 cup / 200g granulated sugar
- 1 cup / 240ml water
- 1 large swath of orange peel
- 1 large swath of lemon peel
- 1 Tbsp kosher salt
- ¼ lime
- 2 oz / 60ml mezcal
- 1 oz / 30ml freshly squeezed lime juice
- 2 dashes of orange bitters

1. To make the simple syrup: Place the sugar and water in a saucepan with the orange peel and lemon peel and bring to a boil. Decrease the heat and simmer for 10 minutes. Cool completely. Discard the peels. Transfer the syrup to a jar with a tight-fitting lid and refrigerate until ready to use or for up to 1 month.
2. Spread the salt on a saucer. Rub the rim of a highball glass with the lime quarter and then dip the rim of the glass in the salt to coat. Fill the glass with ice.
3. In a cocktail shaker, add the mezcal, ¼ cup / 60 ml of the syrup, lime juice, and bitters with 1 cup / 130g ice. Shake and then pour over the ice in the glass.

Appendix 1 Measurement Conversion Chart

Volume Equivalents (Dry)	
US STANDARD	**METRIC (APPROXIMATE)**
1/8 teaspoon	0.5 mL
1/4 teaspoon	1 mL
1/2 teaspoon	2 mL
3/4 teaspoon	4 mL
1 teaspoon	5 mL
1 tablespoon	15 mL
1/4 cup	59 mL
1/2 cup	118 mL
3/4 cup	177 mL
1 cup	235 mL
2 cups	475 mL
3 cups	700 mL
4 cups	1 L

Weight Equivalents	
US STANDARD	**METRIC (APPROXIMATE)**
1 ounce	28 g
2 ounces	57 g
5 ounces	142 g
10 ounces	284 g
15 ounces	425 g
16 ounces (1 pound)	455 g
1.5 pounds	680 g
2 pounds	907 g

Volume Equivalents (Liquid)		
US STANDARD	**US STANDARD (OUNCES)**	**METRIC (APPROXIMATE)**
2 tablespoons	1 fl.oz.	30 mL
1/4 cup	2 fl.oz.	60 mL
1/2 cup	4 fl.oz.	120 mL
1 cup	8 fl.oz.	240 mL
1 1/2 cup	12 fl.oz.	355 mL
2 cups or 1 pint	16 fl.oz.	475 mL
4 cups or 1 quart	32 fl.oz.	1 L
1 gallon	128 fl.oz.	4 L

Temperatures Equivalents	
FAHRENHEIT(F)	**CELSIUS(C) APPROXIMATE)**
225 °F	107 °C
250 °F	120 ° °C
275 °F	135 °C
300 °F	150 °C
325 °F	160 °C
350 °F	180 °C
375 °F	190 °C
400 °F	205 °C
425 °F	220 °C
450 °F	235 °C
475 °F	245 °C
500 °F	260 °C

Appendix 2 The Dirty Dozen and Clean Fifteen

The Environmental Working Group (EWG) is a nonprofit, nonpartisan organization dedicated to protecting human health and the environment Its mission is to empower people to live healthier lives in a healthier environment. This organization publishes an annual list of the twelve kinds of produce, in sequence, that have the highest amount of pesticide residue-the Dirty Dozen-as well as a list of the fifteen kinds ofproduce that have the least amount of pesticide residue-the Clean Fifteen.

THE DIRTY DOZEN	
The 2016 Dirty Dozen includes the following produce. These are considered among the year's most important produce to buy organic:	
Strawberries	Spinach
Apples	Tomatoes
Nectarines	Bell peppers
Peaches	Cherry tomatoes
Celery	Cucumbers
Grapes	Kale/collard greens
Cherries	Hot peppers

The Dirty Dozen list contains two additional itemskale/collard greens and hot peppers-because they tend to contain trace levels of highly hazardous pesticides.

THE CLEAN FIFTEEN	
The least critical to buy organically are the Clean Fifteen list. The following are on the 2016 list:	
Avocados	Papayas
Corn	Kiw
Pineapples	Eggplant
Cabbage	Honeydew
Sweet peas	Grapefruit
Onions	Cantaloupe
Asparagus	Cauliflower
Mangos	

Some of the sweet corn sold in the United States are made from genetically engineered (GE) seedstock. Buy organic varieties of these crops to avoid GE produce.

Appendix 3 Index

ROSEMARIE PIZARRO